The Anxiety Solution

A Quieter Mind, A Calmer You

Chloe Brotheridge, BSc, DipH, DipNLP, HC, is a clinical hypnotherapist and nutritionist who specializes in helping people who suffer from anxiety. Chloe has her own practice in London and has helped hundreds of sufferers overcome severe anxiety.

Having experienced severe anxiety and panic attacks first hand since her teens, and having found her own path to inner healing, Chloe now feels privileged to be able to share with others the transformative tools and techniques she used herself to achieve a sense of control and inner peace.

The Anxiety Solution

A Quieter Mind, A Calmer You

CHLOE BROTHERIDGE

MICHAEL JOSEPH
an imprint of
PENGUIN BOOKS

MICHAEL JOSEPH

UK | USA | Canada | Ireland | Australia
India | New Zealand | South Africa

Michael Joseph is part of the Penguin Random House group of companies
whose addresses can be found at global.penguinrandomhouse.com

Penguin
Random House
UK

First published 2017
003

Copyright © Chloe Brotheridge, 2017

The moral right of the author has been asserted

Set in Garamond MT and Gotham
Typeset by Penguin Books

Printed in Great Britain by Clays Ltd, St Ives plc

A CIP catalogue record for this book is available from the British Library

ISBN: 978–0–718–18715–6

To my family: Mum, Dad, Livi, Charlotte, Granny and Aidan. Thanks for being so wonderful.

Contents

Acknowledgements

A big, huge thank you to the team at Michael Joseph for being so welcoming and lovely. To my editor, Fenella Bates, for your incredible enthusiasm and support from day one. Your positive attitude and excitement about the book was so encouraging.

To Valeria Huerta, my book agent – thank you for everything! I'm forever grateful for all your help and kindness.

To Katy Sunnassee for your smart insights, fantastic editing and being an absolute pleasure to work with. Thank you to Helen Coyle, my copy-editor, for all your incredible help and great work.

Thank you, Mum, for teaching me so much about love and for always being there. Dad, thank you for being the world's wisest, funniest and most patient man. You guys are everything to me.

Thanks to Livi and Charlotte for being such sweethearts. I love you to infinity and beyond.

Thank you to Aidan, my favourite person – for teaching me that 'I am OK', for being my biggest cheerleader and for never saying a mean word, even when you were mad at me!

Thanks to Bonnie S, for simultaneously being the wisest and the most fun person ever, ever, ever. Bonnie B for all the chats, laughs and love. Will for being a great friend, dance partner and bringer of the fun. Josie, thanks for the BEST walks and talks. And to Lucy, I love you!

Thanks to Auntie Vicky and Uncle Ian, who I'll always look up to – for all the advice and encouragement; and to Annie G for all the love and great company.

Thank you to all my clients for being so brave and inspiring and for teaching me so much. Special thanks to those who've allowed me to share their stories in this book.

And finally, thanks to you, the reader. You are amazing, strong, lovable and so, so enough. Please don't forget that! Here's to a Calmer You.

Chloe x

Book Bonuses

Visit www.calmer-you.com/bonus to claim your free bonuses, including audio tracks covering self-hypnosis for relaxation, mindfulness meditation and guided relaxation, plus lots of other useful stuff.

Talking about and sharing your experiences is incredibly important! Join me and other people going through similar things as you in our Facebook group, where you can give and receive support: https://www.facebook.com/groups/calmeryou/

Disclaimer

If you suspect you have anxiety or any other mental health issue, it's essential to speak to your doctor and follow their advice. I also recommend working with a therapist for one-to-one, tailored advice and support. Check with your doctor before starting any exercise or supplement regime.

CHAPTER 1

Let me introduce myself

*When you change the way you look at things,
the things you look at change.*
WAYNE DYER

I've been anxious for as long as I can remember. My parents tell me I was a seriously cautious kid, clinging to the banister as I gingerly made my way down stairs. At ballet classes I would cry in the corner, too inhibited to take part. Although I was confident with people I knew and trusted, talking to new people felt impossible. I feared being told off or making a mistake and dreaded that I would be found out for not being good enough. When something did go wrong – however trivial – I found it hard to cope. On what I thought was my first day at Brownies I discovered that in fact I'd gone on the wrong day and that I wasn't expected. I remember feeling an overpowering sense of shame and embarrassment, as if I'd done something truly awful.

As a young child I had a lot of tantrums and meltdowns. I was a sensitive kid and not very good at handling my own feelings. I was very lucky to have wonderful parents but as the eldest child of three, I felt a lot of pressure to be a 'good girl'. Increasingly, I kept my emotions hidden, so as not to upset Mum, but would then end up having huge, explosive tantrums (usually in public places like shopping centres!).

I first noticed the true signs of anxiety as a teenager. A combination of hormones, deep-seated self-esteem issues, repressed feelings, forays into drinking alcohol and late-night partying culminated in my first panic attack, at the age of fifteen.

During a panic attack your body reacts to what it perceives as a threat. More often than not it's your nervous system overreacting to something that in fact is no threat at all. Triggers can range from giving a speech to too much caffeine, feeling hot and claustrophobic to being overwhelmingly stressed. Sometimes, though, attacks seem to happen for no reason at all. The horrible symptoms – tingling fingers, tight chest, a sensation of impending doom – that feel like a threat to your life, are really the result of your body pumping adrenaline into your muscles so that you can either run away or fight off the threat. In prehistoric times, when predators posed a real danger to mankind, this fight-or-flight response was what would have saved your ass. Nowadays, a journey on the tube or a looming work deadline can trigger the same response, except in these cases, *there's nowhere to run to, and no need.*

My first attack took place at a friend's house. Nothing in particular had triggered it so it was a total shock and I had no idea how to respond. It was the worst feeling of my life. My heart raced and my chest tightened. I literally thought I was dying. (I later discovered that everyone who's experienced a panic attack has the same feeling of dread.) I prayed. I begged my friend to call an ambulance. I genuinely thought, *'this is it'*. The term 'panic attack' hadn't even entered my vocabulary at that age. It wasn't as if we'd learnt about them in school. The only explanation that made any sense to me in my worked up state was that I was having a heart attack and death was *certain*.

That first attack lasted for several hours and only subsided when my body became so exhausted that I was able to fall asleep.

Afterwards I couldn't shake the feeling that my body and brain had let me down and that this uncontrollable *thing* could strike at any moment. I no longer felt safe in my own body. Like many people with anxiety, I became overly focused on how I felt physically, concluding that any changes or new sensations must be a serious problem. What followed was years of anxious feelings and obsessive worrying. I tried to self-medicate with alcohol and food and by attempting to control every detail of my life. Mum eventually suggested I see the college counsellor, whose condescending advice consisted of a chirpy 'Don't panic!' and not a lot else. It took another ten years for me to realize I needed help and to seek professional counselling.

Bouts of anxiety continued when I went to university. It's really hard to enjoy your life when you're locked in a cycle of worry and feel unable to escape. I worried about money, my weight, and that there was something wrong with me. But I didn't want to share my thoughts or feelings with anyone. I'd buried them so deep that it was hard for me to even connect with them, let alone really feel them. If someone had asked me at the time how I felt, I honestly wouldn't have been able to answer – I was numb. And while, on the surface, I seemed to function well, bubbling beneath was a lot of tension, repressed emotion and almost constant overthinking.

Then there was the fact that I'd always felt incredibly uncomfortable and nervous around men, so I found relationships difficult. I'd put on a front and play it cool but inside I was desperately insecure and unable to let anyone in or open up to anybody. It wasn't until I met my current boyfriend, when I was twenty-three, that I learnt to relax enough to be myself and enjoy a relationship.

After university I worked as a nutritionist in the NHS and my primary method for managing anxiety was avoidance. I would stay firmly in my comfort zone with people I knew so that I felt safe. When my friends went on their annual skiing holidays I would stay at home. I was far too afraid to try something so dangerous. I knew things weren't right but I didn't know what to do. I spent three years on and off in counselling, which was invaluable for getting to know myself better, and I had periods when I felt better, but my anxiety never really went away.

Things came to a head when my workload dramatically increased. As well as working full time, I had been training as a hypnotherapist and was now pushing to set up my own therapy practice during the evenings. A cocktail of social media envy – comparing myself unfavourably to other women I felt had achieved so much more than I had – and pressure on myself to 'be better' and 'be more productive', fuelled my deep-seated fear that I would never be good enough. In short, I was burning out. For weeks at a time I would get home at 10 p.m., crawl into bed and cry, my brain and body still buzzing with thoughts about my endless to-do list. I developed Irritable Bowel Syndrome, a condition often associated with anxiety. I was completely miserable. I knew I needed to detox my mind and my life, but I didn't know how.

Then, in 2013, I was at a yoga studio when my attention was drawn to a quote up on the wall. It read, 'Set peace of mind as your highest priority and organize your life around it.' It hit me immediately that this was what I needed to do. 'Being productive' and trying to feel worthy by working hard had been my priority, but it wasn't making me happy. In fact, it was destroying my peace of mind.

Right then, I vowed to make changes. I quit my job in the NHS to focus on my own business. I made meditation and going for walks a non-negotiable part of every day and tried to be kinder to myself, rather than constantly pushing and pressurizing myself. Writing became another cathartic daily practice and I devoured every book I could find on anxiety and personal development. I used my skills as a hypnotherapist and nutritionist to work on my mind and detox my body by cutting out refined carbs and booze. With the space I'd created in my life, and my new kinder-to-me attitude, I began venturing out of my comfort zone to try all the things I had previously been scared to do, in the process teaching myself that I *could* cope.

Needless to say, I felt loads better. It took about six months but it was so worth it. Ironically, I thought that stepping back and being less busy so I could calm my mind would have a detrimental effect on my work. I imagined I would suffer financially, but it turned out that the opposite was true. My work life actually *improved* as my ability to calmly focus and offer the best of myself increased.

For years, I believed that fear and worry were ingrained in my psyche – a permanent part of who I was. Anxiety can amp us into such a fearful state that it's impossible to see a way out. It's exhausting, frustrating and terrifying, like being stuck in a suffocating glass box, feeling sick as you gaze at the world, wondering what it's like to feel 'normal'. I'm here to tell you that it doesn't have to be this way. The truth is, your natural state is one of calmness and confidence – and I'm going to teach you how to get there. We'll explore why we're so anxious in the first place and I'll show you practical ways to detox the rubbish – I'm talking beliefs, behaviours and thought patterns – while adding in lots of positive stuff. I'm going to share all the techniques and insights I used on myself and now use with my clients. You can use them, too, to bring your brain and body back into balance and become your calmest, happiest self.

Throughout the book there are short exercises you can experiment with as you're reading. They're a great way to really understand the more theoretical stuff and begin to work out what works best for you. The final chapter contains the Anxiety Solution Toolkit. This is the in-depth guide to all my tried and trusted self-help techniques. There's space for you to note your own anxiety triggers and a Q&A section covering some of the more common panic-making scenarios, along with suggestions for techniques that might be particularly helpful. The more you interact with this book – trying out the exercises, the meditations and affirmations – the more you will get out of it. It's designed to be inspiring and informative but, above all, practical, so please do throw yourself into doing the work so you can discover for yourself just how powerful these tools really are.

I don't believe in 'curing' anxiety completely. After all, it's a normal human emotion that we all experience from time to time. But I do believe you can strip away the things that detract from your inner peace. You can create a life centred on your own values and goals rather than being swept up in a storm of social media madness, self-imposed pressure and unnecessary worry.

It's time to alight from the anxiety train and begin your new journey towards contentment and clarity. I'm excited for you to get started. Let's go!

CHAPTER 2

Why are we all so worried?

I am an old man and have known a great
many troubles, but most of them have
never happened.

MARK TWAIN

If you suffer from anxiety, then a typical day can feel like one long struggle not to slip into panic. There's a sort of buzz going on in your brain, and its not the good kind. You shower, inhale your breakfast and get the train to work. Your mind is busy in its own internal nightmare. As your tensed-up, crunchy-shouldered body goes through the motions of your day, your brain is set to overthinking autopilot. Your heart races in your chest – a thumping, erratic reminder that you can't cope. Before you even get to the office you've mentally played out today's stressful meeting, felt defensive as you had an argument with your boss about a deadline and sensed a wave of dread wash over you as you imagine tackling that ever-growing mound of emails. Not to mention worrying about everything from sorting out the boiler to creating your own online media empire by the end of the month!

Truth is, all of this happened in your mind as you stood in line at Starbucks.

In our modern world, scenarios such as this have become commonplace. I can guarantee that at least some of those people in the queue with you will be going through the same repetitive thinking. It's becoming the norm for us to feel anxious. We're chronically worried: about cash, our relationship or lack thereof, the housing market, not being good enough, the people we love, whether we'll have babies, what to eat, what not to eat, wars, natural disasters, politics and the economy, the shape and proportions of our bodies and the lines on our faces.

Young women and anxiety

According to the Mental Health Foundation's 2014 report 'Living with Anxiety', 22 per cent of women in the UK feel anxious 'most of the time'.[1] A 2016 review by researchers at Cambridge University found that women are twice as likely to experience anxiety as men, with those under thirty-five most affected.[2] Research has demonstrated that at the age of eleven, boys and girls are equally likely to be anxious but by the time they're fifteen, girls are in the lead.[3]

So what's the explanation for this massive difference in the way women and men experience anxiety? Part of it seems to be down to biology. Women's brains (in particular the amygdala, which governs emotion and responds to stress) are more likely than men's to fire up at a stress-ful event.[4] But there are also a host of social, cultural and political factors that make women particularly prone to anxiety. Women are more likely to experience physical and sexual abuse than men.[5] There is also pressure on women, both from ourselves and society, to 'have it all' – the fantastic career, a great body, a rewarding relationship – and then balance babies, boardrooms, buying property and often taking on the brunt of caring for parents as we, and they, get older. Not to mention the fact that women are paid less than men in 90 per cent of all sectors, accord-ing to the UK government's 2015 report.[6] Then there's the fact that our hormones fluctuate monthly, which can cause more stress and anxiety.

We are also, annoyingly, more likely to ruminate over our problems while men are more likely to take action to solve them.[7] It looks as if this is down to the way we're raised. Dr Lynn Buska of the American Psychological Association told the *Guardian* in 2013, 'As girls, we're taught to think more about relationships and subvert our needs towards the group's needs or towards others. Whereas boys are socialized earlier on to be more assertive and expressive about their needs.'[8] In other words, in order to help lower our stress levels we need to take care of ourselves, express our needs and be a bit more 'selfish'. Taking a more active role in how we cope with things rather than putting up with stress or fretting about it will certainly help. (And if all this sounds daunting, don't worry; this book is stuffed with tips on how to do it!)

A key factor is a sort of 'learnt helplessness' that can result from differences in the way boys and girls are treated by parents, teachers and others. Boys are more often told to 'toughen up' if they slip and fall or make a mistake. Girls are typically given more compassionate attention.

I vividly remember Mum scooping me on to her knee and cooing 'poor baby' – when I was eighteen years old! All because I'd been struggling with something at college. I'm pretty sure she'd respond in the same way now if I scraped my knee. And while this is very loving (thanks, Mum!), it can result in a sense of helplessness. If we're not allowed to discover that we can cope when life feels difficult or things are going wrong, we end up uncertain of our abilities. We don't trust ourselves to be able to fix things, or simply get through them. Many young women have not developed the internal coping mechanisms and confidence to handle challenges.

There's an irony here because we women spend a lot of time trying to hold it all together and, often, we do a very good job of it. At least from the outside. The problem is that even if we're managing pretty well we often fear that we're about to fail. Or we're convinced we're not doing well *enough*. Everywhere I go, whether it's to a party, a work event or a yoga class, when the subject of what I do for a living comes up there will always be at least one woman, often many more, who leans in and, in a hushed voice, confesses her own struggles with anxiety. These women, who appear cool, calm and together, tell me that actually they're a hot mess of worry and self-doubt. There is an epidemic of anxiety happening out there, a lot of it behind closed doors and inside buzzing brains.

How can you tell whether you have anxiety?

When I talk to people about their anxiety they often tell me that they don't want to make a fuss, or that they feel bad because they know there are so many others with worse problems. They believe they ought to be able to pull themselves together. All this puts extra strain on them and makes them feel more anxious.

The first thing to say is that, if you are suffering, then there is a problem and you deserve to get help. If anxiety or worry or panic affect your daily life or are causing you distress, please don't suffer in silence.

If you suspect you may have anxiety it's essential to have it diagnosed by your GP. They will be able to help you decide if therapy or medication is a good option, and also distinguish anxiety from other issues such as depression.

Secondly, all anxiety is normal – you're certainly not 'abnormal' if you have it. Some people experience persistent anxiety no matter what is going on in their lives. For others it's triggered by certain situations such as social events. Other people will experience temporary spells of anxiety, for example when going through a big change in their life or before an exam.

You can't self-diagnose anxiety but, in the interests of

being clear about what we're talking about, it may help you to know that anxiety is basically an umbrella term to describe uncomfortable, nervous thoughts and feelings, often about things in the future. It typically also has physical symptoms, even though it's primarily thought of as a mental health issue. As well as a sense of dread or irritableness and trouble with concentrating, anxiety can make you feel dizzy, sick and exhausted. It can give you palpitations, tense muscles, stomach problems and trouble sleeping. If you've had symptoms such as these for at least six months then your doctor might well diagnose anxiety.

The way that anxiety most typically expresses itself is in worrying. We all worry, of course we do, but if you are thinking about actual or potential problems in a way that regularly creates anxiety, then worry has got out of hand. Worrying is a problem if it feels uncontrollable and stops you from focusing and enjoying life. Maybe you find yourself persistently coming back to the same train of thought again and again. Worry can also be called rumination, over-analysing or overthinking. It's one of the primary symptoms of generalized anxiety disorder (GAD).

The other definite warning sign that something is wrong is if you have feelings of panic. A panic attack is a sudden and overwhelming feeling of intense anxiety caused by a huge rush of adrenaline. You might experience palpitations, shortness of breath (hyperventilation), dizziness, tingling in the fingers, shaking or sweating. Usually the symptoms pass after 5–20 minutes. Panic attacks feel terrifying but they aren't actually dangerous and can't hurt you.

If any of this chimes with you, make an appointment to see your GP right now. *The Anxiety Solution* gives you a whole lot of powerful techniques to manage anxiety and get your life back, but it needs to be used as part of a programme of medical or therapeutic care.

You don't have to stay anxious

If you're one of the millions of people who are suffering, fortunately there is a lot you can do to help yourself. This book is stuffed full of practical suggestions and techniques you can use to manage and diminish your anxiety.

Many of my clients come to me feeling that their anxiety is out of control and that, unless their whole life changes. they will never feel better. I help them to see this is not the case. We *can* make changes to the way we think that allow us to cope with things we previously felt were overwhelming. And it's usually much easier to change ourselves than it is to change our external environment. After all, unless you pack it all in and go and live in a cabin in the woods (and sometimes that might be tempting), then your unreasonable boss is going to remain a fact of life. So is social media. There is no getting away from the need to make decisions, and a certain amount of life stress is inevitable.

Having said all that, it's important and empowering

to remember that you have more options than you may realize. If your relationship is making you miserable, for example, you have the option to leave. If you cry in the loos at work every day, maybe you should hand in your notice. These decisions might cause you anxiety but it's important to remember that, sometimes, changing your external environment is the shortest way out of long-term anxiety.

But whatever our circumstances, if we want to feel better, *we* have to be the ones that change. Only then will our lives change for the better. We have to clean up our thinking and adjust our perspective so we can approach modern life calmly. We may not be able to control everything that goes on in our life, but the good news is that we *do* have control over how we respond to events. When you really grasp the truth of this, the power flows back into your hands.

What causes anxiety?

Anxiety is a natural and normal phenomenon. When human beings were evolving we needed the fight-or-flight response to help us escape from dangers or fight for our lives. These short bursts of adrenaline (and the anxiety and panic they bring with them) kept the species alive. These days, in our society, we live in much safer times. There are no wild bears, and no alien tribes attacking ours. The problem is, the amygdala – the part of the brain that triggers the fight-or-flight response and is responsible for our emotions – didn't get the memo. It misinterprets every-day challenges and irritations – from giving a presentation or flying in an aeroplane to receiving a large bill in the post – as life-or-death situations. Then it fires up our survival response, pouring adrenaline into our blood-stream and making sure we're on high alert. The feeling of nervousness or butterflies in your stomach is a result of your brain directing blood flow away from your diges-tive system and towards your limbs so that you are better able to run away or fight, as required. Excessive worrying is another survival mechanism gone wrong. Worry is designed to help us be on high alert for the worst-case scenario but when it becomes a more or less permanent state of mind, it can profoundly damage our mental health.

That's the general explanation but, of course, some of us are more prone to anxiety than others. The factors that lead to an individual developing anxiety are practi-cally limitless. On its own, knowing the particular events or circumstances that caused you to become anxious probably won't be enough to change how you feel, but self-knowledge can be a powerful first step to lessening the grip anxiety has on your life. It might be that you can't pinpoint the cause of your anxiety. That's also fine. You can still take steps to overcome it.

Here are some possible causes for anxiety:

Genetics plays a role, although genes only ever create a predisposition, they don't *cause* anxiety. In an area of science called epigenetics, scientists have discovered that your lifestyle, your behaviours and diet can make genes either turn on or off. So even if you think you might have inherited a predisposition towards anxiety, there is a lot you can do to help yourself.

Childhood and upbringing definitely play a part. As children, we are very impressionable and we learn ways of thinking, feeling and behaving from observing family members and from our experiences. Perhaps you had an anxious parent and you learnt to worry by copying them. Or you might have had a critical parent for whom nothing was ever good enough. From this you learnt to be overly self-critical or a perfectionist. Or maybe being overprotected meant you grew up without learning how to cope with challenges on your own.

Stressful life events and trauma in your past can affect your current situation. Things such as your parents' acrimonious divorce, the death of someone close to you, experiencing abuse or being involved in an accident can all be highly stressful and traumatic experiences that leave you feeling unsafe, fearful and uncertain. In this context, anxiety is partly a protection mechanism to try to keep you safe in the future. You may have taken on board the belief that you must worry or be on high alert in order to be safe. Even seemingly less significant things such as a humiliating experience at school could contribute to anxiety.

Your lifestyle is a huge and often underestimated factor. Not taking care of yourself, not getting enough sleep, eating poorly and not taking any exercise could lead to or make anxiety worse.

Long-term health problems or chronic pain can contribute to anxiety.

Big life changes such as getting a new job, buying a house, getting married or experiencing a break-up could cause an increase in stress that leads to anxiety.

Alcohol or drug use or abuse or side effects from some prescription drugs can bring on anxiety or make it worse.

Whatever the causes of your anxiety, please remember: it's not your fault and you're not stuck with it. Change is always possible. In fact, change is inevitable because nothing stays the same and, as human beings, learning and progress is innate to us. You can do this.

Are we getting more anxious?

The latest research shows that a higher proportion of young people are reporting mental health problems (including anxiety) than ever before. But does this mean that anxiety is more of an issue, or is it simply a more recognized condition?

It's been suggested that millennials (born 1980–2000) have grown up with some new factors that might account for their sky-high anxiety levels. They are often described as the 'over-protected generation'. Generational demographer Neil Howe characterizes their baby-boomer parents as 'helicopter parents', hovering over their children, ready to intervene – or interfere! – should the child need anything. Studies have linked helicopter parenting with increased rates of anxiety and depression in children.[9]

Being close to our parents is a wonderful thing, but the flip side of that closeness is that we may be unable to function as adults ourselves, preferring to defer responsibility to authority figures when we're stuck. And our parents' fear can rub off on us. If you've been warned to 'be careful!' often enough, it's easy to grow up thinking the world is a dangerous place. Due to a psychological phenomenon called 'confirmation bias', you're likely to unconsciously seek out evidence for the things you believe are true. If, unconsciously, you are sure that potential tragedy lurks around every corner, your brain scans your environment for evidence to support this. It can mean you're constantly on high alert, expecting something bad to happen. This plays havoc with your stress response. When your adrenal glands are producing too much cortisol – one of the stress hormones – you end up feeling permanently anxious.

Another big problem with being overprotected is that

our failures are prevented before they've even happened. We are the first generation to grow up with mobile phones, which means that parental advice and support are never more than a few seconds away. But if you don't feel able to make decisions alone, if you've been protected from making mistakes or experiencing rejection, you won't have learnt that failure is OK and that you can overcome setbacks. The result is a fear that if something bad does happen, you won't be able to deal with it. The truth is than you are stronger, wiser and more capable that you think. This book will teach you to trust yourself more, so a lot of that anxiety will fall away. Again, all these things are learnt, not innate, which means you can unlearn them.

The trouble with social media

It's been suggested that another reason for the increase in anxiety among young people might be that we are the first generation to have grown up with social media. Never before in history have we known so much about what other people have, do and look like, from their perfectly arranged breakfast bowl of oats and acai berries to their 'effortless' bikini bodies, as evidenced by a string of sweaty-yet-sexy gym selfies. What we see in the media and online is a constant stream of carefully curated shots of fabulous holidays, amazing career achievements and yoga-honed bodies. It can end up adding fuel to the fire of self-doubt and perfectionism when we compare our lives, and bodies, to others. Because, for most of us, our biggest fear is that we are *not good enough*.

Being constantly connected to social media can become addictive. Research says we check our phones up to eighty-five times a day.[10] That's a lot of potential for added stress and information overload, not to mention envy and dissatisfaction with our own lives. But why are we so hooked on our screens? The answer is probably that dopamine is involved. This neurochemical causes us to seek out 'a hit' of gossip, information or news. And, by the way, it triggers the same neural pathways as cocaine and nicotine: the struggle is real.

For me, there is a direct correlation between the number of times I check my phone and the speed of my thoughts. Every bit of information has the potential to create a cascade of feelings, memories and stress. I've been known to be *that girl* who checks her emails before getting out of bed, and it only takes one urgent email to get the adrenaline pumping before I've even brushed my teeth.

A couple of years ago I made a resolution to reduce my use of social media. I'm glad I did, because a 2015 study by the Happiness Research Institute in Denmark proved that social media is making us miserable.[11] It found that those who abandoned Facebook for a week were happier, less worried and less stressed than those who continued to log in.

Think of the media you consume as being like food for your brain and soul. If you feed your brain junk, you're going to feel like crap, end of story. If you want to feel good, a digital detox might be a good idea to cleanse out all the rubbish. Social media isn't all bad, of course, and it's pretty much impossible to avoid it completely, but there are ways to limit it, shift your perspective on it and build yourself up so it doesn't mess with your peace of mind or self-worth.

Are you hooked on worrying?

There's nothing nice about feeling anxious, right? Worrying is one of the most unpleasant ways to spend your time. That's absolutely true, but (here's a biggie that could be keeping you stuck) many people believe, consciously or unconsciously, that their worry serves a purpose. How often have you thought things such as:

'If I worry about work enough, it will motivate me to work harder.'

'If I imagine {insert catastrophic disaster} happening, at least I'll be mentally prepared for the worst.'

'If I have a freak out about money, it will help me to come up with a solution to get me out of this mess.'

'If I punish myself by worrying about that mistake I made, it will stop me from making it again.'

If you believe that worrying serves a useful purpose, it's much harder to stop doing it. I should know. I used to think it helped. I felt compelled to worry, convinced it was useful in some way that I couldn't quite rationalize. Sometimes it felt like my way of trying to find a 'perfect' solution to a problem. Other times, worry was simply my default setting; if my mind started to wander or if I was without distractions, worry would be there, taking the reins and veering off into some horrible places. On some level I felt it wasn't safe to relax in case something went wrong. I had to be on high alert.

If you're worrying as a way to try to solve your problems, then you need to know that it's highly unlikely to give you any valuable insight. This might be hard to swallow if you're a habitual worrier, but I assure you it's true. When you're chronically worried you're almost always stuck in a state of confusion, panic and fear, caught in a jumble of thoughts and emotions that has you tied up in knots. This frenzied state is light years away from the calm clarity that leads to true insight. When we're clear-headed, we're better able to focus, solve problems and tune in to our inner resources and strengths. The truth is, you are more prepared to handle things when you're relaxed and living in the moment.

Maybe you believe that worrying motivates you to do better. Surely all that worry will make you try harder next time? In fact, the opposite is true. Studies have shown that giving ourselves a hard time is strongly linked with lower levels of motivation and increased procrastination.[12] In fact, being kind and supportive to ourselves is what truly motivates us.[13] Say you've been trying to exercise more. You spend your time worrying about how unfit you're getting, how useless you are and how you *simply must make time to exercise*. The more you worry about it, the less appealing it seems. You feel shitty about the whole thing and end up ordering a curry and zoning out in front of Netflix. Worry saps your motivation and your mental energy to do the things you want to do.

But *surely* worry is helpful sometimes? I hear you ask. True. In the very short term, a little worry can be just the thing to light a fire under your bum and get you to take action. But those chronic, circular worries about uncontrollable future events? They aren't doing you any good. (And if some part of you secretly believes that worrying about things will stop them from happening, I'm here to tell you to let that one go, once and for all!)

You're not alone with your anxiety

One of the things that can keep us feeling stuck in anxiety is a sense of deep alienation from those around us. For people who have never experienced anxiety, it can be difficult to understand. Incredulous partners and friends may say things like, 'Why can't you just snap out of it?' They won't understand why you're getting so worked up over something that, to them, is trivial, and they'll not have a clue that you lie awake most nights as a tiny army of *'what ifs'* march through your brain, becoming more irrational as the hours tick on. After all, it's tough to understand unless you've been there, felt the gut-wrenching dread and been practically paralysed by endless rumination.

But when people don't understand what we're going through it leaves us feeling lonely and can make us doubt ourselves. Perhaps they're right and we *should* just snap out of it? Then we end up feeling guilty and ashamed for not being able to cope, or for making a fuss about things when other people have it so much worse. We can see how lucky we are to have enough to eat and a roof over our head and to live in a stable country with no wars or natural disasters, so we feel guilty for still finding so many things to worry about.

If this sounds familiar, please give yourself a break. There's actually an explanation for this phenomenon of there always being a new thing to worry about. It's called Maslow's hierarchy of needs. Abraham Maslow was a psychologist and came up with his groundbreaking theory back in 1943. He claimed that we all have needs which we are constantly trying to meet. The most basic and crucial ones are for things like food and shelter because, unless they are met, we will die. Once we've dealt with those, we move on to safety, which includes things like good health and personal security. The next tier of needs covers friendship, intimacy and family; then comes esteem and respect. Finally, once we've taken care of everything else, comes self-actualization. That's the fun stuff about finding your purpose, uncovering your passions and living the fullest life you possibly can.

In modern times in our culture, many of us are lucky enough to have our basic needs met, which is clearly great. But that simply opens us up to new levels of things to worry about. Things such as our achievements, what other people think of us, what we think of ourselves, our creative pursuits, what we look like or reaching our full potential. Yes, we're in an incredibly privileged position to be able to worry about these things, but it's all relative and your feelings *are* valid. It's normal, as more of your needs are met, that the things which concern you will change.

All this shame and guilt mean that it's no surprise that, according to a 2010 survey by Anxiety UK, 55 per cent of us don't feel comfortable telling others about our anxiety.[14] This sense of isolation and stigma has serious consequences. It is very often one of the reasons people don't get help. Another study found that only 15–25 per cent of people with some kind of anxiety actually get treatment for it.[15]

Please remember that you are not unusual if you suffer from anxiety. The statistics suggest that 22 per cent of us suffer from it. Don't let your feelings of isolation or guilt around not being able to cope stop you from seeking help. As well as speaking to your GP, try contacting one of the organizations listed in the back of the book. There is a lot of support out there.

Reasons to be cheerful

A seriously reassuring study recently found that 85 per cent of the things we worry about actually end up having *positive* outcomes and 79 per cent of people coped better than they thought they would when things didn't go to plan.[16] I'm sure you've had the experience of dreading something beforehand – a party or a meeting – and imagining all the things that could go wrong, only to find that in reality it goes well and you actually enjoy yourself. Things will probably turn out fine and, even if they don't, you'll handle them better than your anxious mind thought you could.

Here's something else that happens when we're worried. We get confused about *probability* and *possibility*. When we turn on the news, it's easy to think that the world is a dangerous place. Fear-mongering stories grab people's attention and drive up ratings. We're all glued to our phones, so the intricate details of the latest world horror are only ever a few clicks away. Those things are, of course, sadly real. But because it's only the bad stuff that is reported in the media, our perception about the *probability* of something terrible happening is skewed. There is always that possibility but the probability is very small.

You might find it reassuring to know that, despite all the doom and gloom, in the media it simply isn't true that the world is on the decline and suffering is at its peak. The data says differently. The website Our World in Data[17] shows us that the world has never been a safer, richer, healthier place. There is less poverty, fewer homicides, fewer wars and more democracy than ever before. Average life expectancy in the UK has gone from thirty-four years in 1543 to eighty-two in the year 2012. For the majority of us there has never been a better, safer time to be alive.

I want you to consider that people have coped with things for millennia. You and your DNA are the result of 200,000 years of natural selection during which only the toughest, smartest and most resilient humans survived to make babies. You are a refined and brilliant human being. You're, basically, amazing. Don't underestimate your abilities and resources. You already have all the abilities and strengths to survive and be happy. It's built into your human-ness. *Believing* you are capable is the only thing you need to do to actually *be* capable.

I remember talking to my mum a few years ago about childbirth. I was pretty anxious about the whole idea of pushing a tiny human out of me (we've all heard the 'pulling a chicken out of your nose' equivalence stories, haven't we?!) and all the pain, blood and *potential* danger involved. What she told me changed the way I thought about it for ever. She explained that there is an intelligence and wisdom in the human body that knows what to do, a part of you that was passed down from mother to daughter through every generation. It's instinctual. It's innate. We contain resources we're not necessarily even conscious of which we can call upon when we need them most. We can absolutely trust ourselves to know what to do when that moment of birth comes because it's in our DNA. This is true of any situation in life.

If all this sounds too good to be true, don't worry! This book is full of strategies that will support you in worrying less. It takes practice, but you can do it. For now, I want you to just hold this thought: your anxiety is not your destiny. You are way more powerful than you realize and you will get past it.

Summary

★ Young women are particularly vulnerable to anxiety but there are lots of things you can do to help yourself.

★ If you suspect you are suffering from anxiety, make an appointment with your GP or contact a support group such as MIND. Don't self-diagnose your anxiety.

★ Anxiety is never your fault. Neither is it an innate part of who you are. Change is possible.

★ Don't let guilt, shame or fear stop you from getting help for your anxiety. You are not alone and you *can* get better.

★ You are a brilliant human being and way more capable than you think!

CHAPTER 3

Anxiety: your biggest teacher

Turn your wounds into wisdom.

OPRAH WINFREY

I know the idea of there being anything positive about anxiety is highly counter-intuitive, but stay with me. Because here's the truth: anxiety is a messenger and it's calling out for you to pay attention. It wants you to learn something, change something, understand something or heal something. If you dig below the surface of your anxious symptoms, there's often a belief or experience at their root, or a need that's not being met. When you stop being afraid of your anxiety and turn the fear into curiosity, you can recognize what it's trying to teach you. That way, you can shift it for good and often deal with the deeper unresolved issue in the process.

The problem is that, mostly (and kind of understandably), we just want our anxiety to go away as quickly and painlessly as possible. We ignore it. We try to keep going, hoping it will resolve itself. Or we tell ourselves that, if we stay busy enough, we won't have to feel it. We paper over it with medication, work, sex, alcohol or the thrill of another achievement, but the anxiety keeps resurfacing until we eventually learn to meet our needs.

There is a shortcut. If we welcome anxiety and treat it as a friend or a teacher, it can help us to learn something about ourselves. Paradoxically, embracing our anxiety can be the quickest way to live a less anxious life.

My anxiety was trying to teach me a number of things. Firstly, and perhaps most fundamentally, to be more open and accepting of myself; to love myself and know that I was worthy of love. Until a few years ago I felt I had to hide the real me since no one could possibly like me if they knew what I was really like. At school I always felt like an outsider. My parents were from the south of England but had moved to the north when I was little. We were tall, skinny vegetarians living in a northern town famous for its love of meat pies. I was one of the tallest people in my year, ate 'weird' food and spoke with a funny accent. I desperately needed to fit in so I would save all my pocket money to buy the latest tracksuit jackets, trying to look like everyone else, but they never seemed to fit my abnormally long arms. I would turn bright red when my English teacher put me on the spot to answer a question. I felt wrong, as if I didn't fit. I was different, and terrified of being seen for who I was.

I started dating and chose men who were either emotionally unavailable or mirrored back to me the same lack of respect I had for myself. When I met my current boyfriend, when I was twenty-three, the relationship was initially filled with anxiety. I was a bottomless pit of neediness, super insecure and desperate for love and reassurance. I would often get sick with jealousy. All my thoughts and feelings expressed my need for love but I wanted it all from another person – from him. So when my boyfriend pointed out that perhaps if I loved *myself* a bit more I wouldn't be so anxious and unstable, it was a revelation – I'd never considered doing that! Surely loving yourself was arrogant and self-centred?

In fact, it was *exactly* what I needed to do. I hadn't realized that having a healthy level of self-respect was an essential component of a calm and happy life.

From that moment I slowly began to learn, day by day, that I would continue to feel insecure for as long as I sought security outside of myself, because external things – and that includes other people – are, essentially, outside of our control. But when love, acceptance and security come from within us, we always have enough. Only *I* could meet my own need for love, and the same goes for you. We all have within us a limitless supply of love. My anxiety was pointing me towards learning to *be* that source of love for myself and to learn that I am OK, regardless of what other people think of me.

Another thing I've learnt from befriending my anxiety is to allow myself to try things and be bad at them. Previously, I would only ever do things I knew I could do well, which kept me stuck in a comfort zone. Anxiety stopped me growing for fear of making a fool of myself. But I've learnt that I don't need to be perfect at everything and that experiencing discomfort doesn't mean I can't still move forward and do what I set out to do. I needn't let feeling scared hold me back.

A major lesson I've learnt from anxiety, one that I continue to work on, is to s-l-o-w d-o-w-n and take care of myself. Walking, eating, working, whatever – I always wanted to do it all *fast*! Many of us have a tendency to want to rush, to overwork, over-push, over-pressurize and over-caffeinate to keep going. Our bodies, brains and nervous systems aren't designed for this kind of pressure over the long term, so eventually they push back. Tense shoulders, a racing heart, a dodgy tummy and panic attacks can all stem from trying to do too much. All these symptoms were alarm bells telling me I needed to change my lifestyle, urgently.

So I made time for the important stuff: meditation, exercise and chatting on the phone to people I loved. Nowadays, if I find myself trying to push too hard, my body always lets me know. The difference is that, now, I listen. Yours will shout louder and louder until you listen, too. What's it saying right now? Maybe it's trying to tell you that life isn't a race and you're not trying to get any-where; in fact, you're already where you need to be.

My client Annabel, thirty-nine, works in the City. For years she was a workaholic, always rushing from place to place, never giving herself a chance to rest and process things. There was always something to worry about, from forgetting to turn off the hob before she left for work to big stuff, such as the health of her family. She was tired but wired. Her adrenaline levels were consistently high and she would get to the end of the day feeling exhausted and overwhelmed but unable to sleep.

A big part of our work together was focused on figuring out what Annabel's anxiety was trying to communicate to her. She realized that her need for balance was not being met and that she had to work on her lifestyle. Issues around low self-worth were pushing her to overwork and overachieve in order to feel worthwhile. She needed to build more rest into her day and start setting boundaries with people. Slowing down helped her to feel less overwhelmed so that she could finally trust herself to handle things.

· ·

Exercise: learning from anxiety

Sit down, take some deep breaths and close your eyes. With every out breath, feel yourself relaxing deeper into your chair. When you're relaxed, ask yourself, 'What is this anxiety trying to teach me? What does it want me to learn, change or do?' Some examples might be: to love yourself more, to slow down, to take care of yourself, to stand up for yourself, to set boundaries, to step up and do the things you're scared to do, to take life less seriously, to trust yourself, to let go, to take action, or to walk away from a situation. Listen closely for what things come to mind for you and write them down in a notebook.

· ·

Changing the broken record

Anxiety is sometimes the result of replaying unresolved emotional pain from the past, like a record that's stuck on repeat. Almost all of us (scrap that, *all* of us!) have an issue that could do with being resolved. None of us comes out of childhood unscathed. When we're young we're like sponges, absorbing experiences, things we're told and things that we see other people doing. But when we're too young to fully understand the situations and behaviours we're witnessing, we often give them incorrect meanings. We end up arriving at the wrong conclusions.

I had a client, Claire, twenty-two, whose dad had had an affair and left the family when she was eight years old. Much of her anxiety centred on the fear that she was unlovable and would always be abandoned. She had misinterpreted her dad leaving as being her fault. She would worry constantly when she was in a relationship, feeling insecure, tense and terrified. The anxiety was a symptom of something deeper, a signpost pointing towards pain from the past that needed to be healed.

I asked Claire to visualize her eight-year-old self and to stand alongside her. Claire told her younger self that Dad leaving was not her fault, that he really did love her but was acting the way he did because of his own issues and his own pain. She gave her younger self a big hug and reassured her that things would be OK. This is a powerful exercise for resolving pain in the past and changing negative self-beliefs.

. . . .

Exercise: helping 'little you'

Imagine you're standing alongside your younger self at a time when you really needed some love and support. Explain to her the things she doesn't understand at this point in her life. Is there anything she needs to know? What does she need to learn? What words of encouragement, love and support can you give her? If you want to, you can imagine someone else there to help you – a wise soul offering advice. What would they say about this situation? Now imagine giving your younger self a big hug and telling her that everything is going to be all right. Make some notes about the things you said and re-read them often.

. . . .

You won't be anxious for ever

When you befriend your anxiety and accept that it has valuable lessons to teach you, you take the fundamental first step to an anxiety-free life. The next thing to take on board is that change is possible. You are not an intrinsically anxious person. You can totally do this!

For a start, anxiety is not solely genetic. Genetic factors can cause a predisposition for anxiety but it's your experiences and lifestyle that have the biggest impact on whether or not you suffer from it. Traumatic or stressful events, having anxious parents or not taking proper care of yourself can all cause you to feel anxious. The good news is that most of the reasons you're anxious are learnt, which means you can unlearn them.

Even deeply distressing experiences don't have to stay with you for ever. An interesting study done on rats discovered that rodents deprived of maternal love and attention became more anxious as adults. But this anxiety was reversible.[1] Your genetic predisposition or early childhood experiences *can* be overcome.

So your anxiety is not a hard-wired part of who you are. In fact, you have a huge amount of power to change your brain's wiring for the better. Up until recently, it was thought that the brain's structure was fixed, but scientists now agree that our experiences in life reorganize our neural pathways. For example, London taxi drivers have to memorize the names of every street in the city. This leads to an enlargement of the hippocampus, the area in the brain responsible for visual-spatial memory. People who regularly meditate change the structure of their brain in positive ways, too. If we choose carefully what we think, say and do on a regular basis, we can actually forge new mental pathways to favour more optimistic, uplifted and positive thoughts.[2]

But you needn't become a cabbie or a Buddhist nun to change your brain for the better. Exercise and socializing are two simple activities that have been found to change the way your brain handles stress because, when you're in interesting and stimulating environments, your brain creates new pathways and becomes more resilient as a result.

Change your mindset with meditation

One of the easiest ways to begin to change your neural pathways for the better and to calm an anxious mind is with meditation. It's been around for centuries and for good reason – it works! If you're not already a seasoned meditator, you might think of it as 'airy fairy, New Age, ain't-nobody-got-time-for-that' type stuff. As one of my clients recently said, 'One step too hippy for me.' Or maybe it's something you wish you could do, if only you could sit cross-legged long enough and shut out all your thoughts. I can relate. I used to think exactly the same way.

In the seventies Mum and Dad were caught up in the hippy movement. The day they met, Dad had shoulder-length hair and was wearing bright red flared corduroy trousers. Straight away my mum knew he was The One. They were juicing before juicing was *en vogue* and meditation for them was a daily practice. Fast-forward a few years to me as an anxious teenager . . . and I really could have benefited from doing the meditation Mum suggested I do. The only problem was I'd already *found* my inner peace. And it lived at the bottom of a blue alcopop bottle.

Whenever I tried to meditate I got frustrated by the

torrent of thoughts that kept coming in, and having to sit in silence only made me even more aware of the anxious tightness in my chest or the pounding of my heart. I would, however, get glimpses of the power of meditation when I suddenly felt myself drifting into a deeper part of myself where things felt quieter and calmer. The problem was that I was using meditation as an occasional tool to try to calm extreme nerves or panic. And as anyone who's ever tried to sit still and calm the mind when they're panicking will know, this just doesn't work. I just *knew* meditation wasn't for me.

What I later learnt is that meditation is far more than a relaxation tool. Yes, it's a great way to calm yourself and relax, which is essential when you're anxious. But it's also a tool for changing the structure and function of your brain, to make you more positive and happy. It's something that needs to be done regularly to reap the benefits, rather than every so often.

In about 2010 I began to dabble again in meditation. I would do it regularly for a few weeks and, lo and behold, I would feel better. But then – as so many of us do with new habits – I got cocky, thinking I no longer needed it. I gave it up. A few weeks later I had slipped back into feeling stressed out and worried again. This cycle continued for months.

When I finally started meditating regularly, in 2013, it was nothing short of game-changing. Up until that point I used to tell myself things like, 'Who's got time to meditate?! I've got shit to do!' I was convinced I didn't even have time for a lunch break, let alone to meditate. It seemed like a luxury. A waste of time that I just couldn't justify.

But by then I had realized that there's no point in being productive or even 'successful' if you're miserable and anxious. There's also no point in being busy if the work you produce is below par because you're so frazzled and tense that your best stuff doesn't get a chance to shine through. I really wanted to help other people to become less anxious, and it finally dawned on me that the best thing I could do to help others was to help myself first. These days I think of meditation as being as essential as showering – like a daily cleansing for the nervous system! It's literally that high up on my list of priorities.

I had feared that meditating would take away time from my work and my social life. Part of me worried that I would fall behind and nothing would ever get done. Actually, I found that the opposite was true. I was able to work with calm focus, meaning I got more done with less stress. Creativity just seemed to flow more easily and, because I was more at peace with myself, my connection with friends and my boyfriend seemed to get better. For me, meditation is the antidote to the ills of modern life.

I'm not the only one. Meditation has helped dozens of my clients prove to themselves that they have the power to literally rewire their own brains to make them a happier place to be. My client Nadia, twenty-six, who works in sales, uses meditation to calm herself and has found it totally life-changing. 'I'm just sorry I didn't try it earlier because, now, I'm a total convert. It has changed my mindset completely. If I stop doing it for more than a few days my mood unravels and anxieties creep back in. But as long as I do ten minutes every day, I know I can stay calm.'

You'll find out more about meditation, how it can help and how to do it in the Anxiety Solution Toolkit in Chapter nine. But for now, if you're telling yourself, 'I don't have time to meditate,' instead, ask yourself, 'Do I have time to feel anxious and unhappy?'

Summary

★ You have the power to make anxiety a totally manageable part of your life.

★ Many of the reasons for anxiety are learnt, and you *can* unlearn them, even if genetic factors or traumatic or stressful events have affected you.

★ Meditation is one of the single most powerful tools you have to rewire your brain to make it less prone to anxiety.

★ With as little as ten minutes focused practice a day you can be well on your way to bringing your anxiety under control.

CHAPTER 4

Boosting self-esteem

To be beautiful means to be yourself. You don't
need to be accepted by others. You need to
accept yourself.

THICH NHAT HANH, BUDDHIST MONK

Until a couple of years ago it didn't matter to me what I'd achieved in any one day – it never felt like enough. There was always more to do, more to achieve, there were more pressing items on my to-do list. I didn't think I deserved relaxation time. I would feel guilty if I took the evening off to watch a film, telling myself I should be doing something productive. I put so much pressure on myself that I would either overwork until I was a head-achey, tense mess or spiral the other way, procrastinating on the web for hours, unable to tackle anything because the self-imposed pressure made me too anxious.

I've spoken to a lot of women about this; it comes up time and time again. I believe one of the biggest sources of our anxiety is the feeling of not *doing* or *being enough*. It's as if we all believe that anything less than perfect is rubbish. This belief is often at the root of why we push ourselves so hard and give ourselves such a mental beating. But if you allow yourself to feel that you are *already* good enough, you can just do your best, knowing that it's always enough.

Of course, there may be very real pressures on you right now. But if you're really honest, much of the time it's pressure you put on yourself. Whether it's to be successful, achieve a goal, look a certain way or please other people, there's a belief that once you achieve it, whatever it is, *then* you'll be happy. People often sacrifice their happiness and wellbeing in the moment and create a tonne of pressure and anxiety, believing it will lead to happiness at some point in the future.

But this isn't how life works. In his book *The Happiness Advantage*, Shawn Achor discusses the way many of us put off happiness until we're 'successful'. How many times have you said to yourself, 'Once I get that promotion / lose 10 lbs / move to a bigger house, then I'll be happy'? But Shawn's studies suggest that we should be thinking about this the other way around. When we put our happiness first, it actually enables us to be more successful. 'When we are positive, our brains become more engaged, creative, motivated, energetic, resilient and productive at work,' says Shawn. (You'll learn how to put your happiness first and super-charge your positivity in the Anxiety Solution Toolkit in Chapter nine.)

In the battle against perfectionism it's also crucial to live according to your own values and not to let anyone else's definition of success rule your life. Ask yourself,

'Is what I'm striving for what I really want?' Author and self-help guru for the modern woman, Gabrielle Bernstein, encourages us to measure our 'success' by how much fun we're having. What if that was your priority, rather than whatever the media or society is currently claiming represents success? What if you measured your achievements in happiness, peace of mind and fun? Imagine for a moment what *that* would be like? It is possible – it's your life and you are in control, no one else.

Supercharge your self-esteem

Self-esteem refers to how you think and feel about yourself and how you value your own opinions and rate your worth. Confidence and self-esteem are two different things. Confidence refers to your belief in your ability to do something. It's possible to be an outwardly confident person – being happy to speak in public or to wear super-short shorts, for example – but inside to suffer from crippling self-esteem issues. I'll talk more about how to improve your confidence levels in Chapter six, but for now, let's focus on self-esteem.

Self-esteem is really important when it comes to your anxiety levels. Healthy self-esteem doesn't mean thinking you're perfect; just the opposite – it means loving yourself, faults and all. In fact, it is a super important ally when it comes to facing down perfectionism. If your self-esteem is fragile, you're less likely to be able to handle criticism and bounce back after disappointments. It can also stop you from taking care of yourself and can hold you back from trying new things. When you have low self-esteem you are extra vulnerable to falling into the trap of thinking that, since you clearly aren't perfect, you must be useless. You take criticism, rejection or mistakes as further proof of your lack of value. This feeling of not being good enough can create a lot of anxiety.

A client recently said to me, 'I know there are so many things I should be doing that would be good for me, such as meditation or exercise, but I don't feel I'm worth taking care of.' This really broke my heart. If we don't feel we're worth it, it makes sense that it's hard to take care of ourselves. When we know our own value, though, it becomes second nature. And when we're prioritizing self-care we feel more supported and able to handle life's ups and downs.

The problem with self-esteem

In the seventies there was a 'self-esteem movement'. Experts told parents that the key to raising happy kids was to boost their self-esteem, no matter what. In an attempt to ensure that children felt great about themselves, many parents and teachers told them how smart, brilliant and perfect they were. But this approach, however well intentioned, can really backfire. My client Anna, twenty-six, told me, 'I was treated like a princess and told I was special; more intelligent and beautiful than other children.' Her family wanted her to feel good about herself – and yes, she was a great kid – but the idea of specialness and perfection wasn't based on reality. (It never is, since perfection doesn't exist.) When she went to university Anna discovered she wasn't the smartest person there, or the prettiest either. Her artificially inflated self-esteem was crushed and she felt terrible about herself as a result.

That's why it's important to build your self-esteem on solid ground, on things that are real. And not only that but to work on self-compassion, too – recognizing yourself as imperfect and human but worthy and good enough just as you are. The good news is that you have loads of genuine reasons to feel good about yourself. Check out the four exercises in the following pages to start building up your self-worth.

Building your self-worth

In his book *Feeling Good*, psychiatrist Dr David Burns, a cognitive-behavioural-therapy (CBT) expert, asked one of his clients to draw a line on a piece of graph paper showing her 'worth' over time. She drew a squiggled line that dipped when she lost her job and again when she gained weight and rose a little when she got a promotion and then a new boyfriend. Afterwards, David took the pen and drew a straight line across the graph paper. She may have believed that she was worth less when she didn't have a job or a boyfriend but he wanted to demonstrate to her that she was always valuable and worthwhile.

Your worth is not dependent on external things. It doesn't fluctuate, no matter what you do or don't do. It isn't tied to how productive you are. Think about it: if someone you love is unwell, or elderly, or has decided to quit the nine-to-five to travel the world, they may not be being 'productive' in terms of work but they are no less loved and valuable to you. Even if you did nothing all day you would still be valuable. As a human being, you are worthwhile just for being you.

It's also important to remember that you've always done your best. It's often said that we're all 'doing the best we can with the tools and resources we have at the time'. The truth is, if you'd had tools or resources or insights to have done things better or differently in the past, then you would have. Maybe you've used the fact that you have anxiety as another reason to give yourself a hard time. Anxiety is flippin' hard enough without adding an extra layer of guilt into the mix. When you're anxious, beating yourself up over perceived mistakes can feel like a full-time occupation. You might tell yourself you should be better, should be over it or shouldn't feel the way you feel. Don't 'should' all over yourself! From now on, banish all those 'shoulds' and be kind to yourself.

You have intrinsic worth just for being you. This is enough. You are not broken, deficient or lacking in any way. It's a bloody miracle that we human beings exist at all, evolving out of stardust over five billion years. Just

47

think, you're one of the most complex and beautiful beings in the universe! You have always been and will always be enough. Remind yourself of this until you believe it because, I promise you, it's true.

. . . .

Exercise: change your perspective

See yourself through the eyes of someone who loves you. Imagine them standing in front of you. Then float up out of yourself and into their shoes. See yourself through their eyes. Feel with their heart. Hear with their ears. See the things that they see in you: your smile, your amazing sense of humour, your unique style, your beautiful mind and the quirks that make you the gorgeous, lovable woman that you are. From their perspective, tell yourself everything you need to know to understand how loved and valued you are. Send a warm glow back to yourself, then float back into your body and receive that love and appreciation.

. . . .

Exercise: zoom in on the positives

Focus on the things you like about yourself – do you make your friends laugh like nothing else? Are you a fantastic baker? Do you pick really thoughtful gifts for people? Do you have a legendary sense of direction? Have you overcome a big challenge and bounced back? Did you get some great feedback at your last work review? Did you do something awesome lately to help someone? Focusing on the things you appreciate and like about yourself reminds you of all the ways that you're a worthwhile, valuable person. Remember, you don't have to be 'special' or be 'the best' to be valuable. You're valuable already! I'd like to challenge you to write a list of fifty things you like about yourself and refer back to the list often. You can also try creating a 'jar of awesome'. On bits of paper, write down compliments you've been given, things you've done well, challenges you've handled, positive thoughts you've had about yourself, achievements you've had and times you helped other people. Put them all into a jam jar and fish a few out to read whenever you need a boost.

• •

Exercise: **do what you love**

Discover your strengths and the things you're good at – and go and do them. Nothing gives us a self-esteem boost more than doing an activity we enjoy and that we're good at. If you're great at singing, belt out a song. If you're amazing at planning parties and events, go and plan one! Does writing light you up? Start that blog or book you've been thinking about. Do you love to travel and organize trips? Get one booked in. (Also, can I come?) You have many gifts and strengths and I truly believe it's your life's purpose to find out what they are and have fun doing them. Being good at stuff and doing what we love gives us a serious boost.

. . . .

Exercise: review your relationships

Is it time to do a relationship audit? Look at who you spend most time with. Do they build you up or drag you down? Maybe you're in a relationship with someone who doesn't support you, or you have a friend who's always competing against you or letting you down. It might be the moment to start being more assertive with these people, or to let them go completely. I know this is easier said than done, but you deserve to be surrounded by people who love, support and believe in you, so have a good think about the people in your life that add to it and those who don't. Maybe it's about setting boundaries with people and letting them know what is and isn't OK with you. When you set a boundary you're making an important statement to yourself and other people that you value yourself.

And remember, basing your self-esteem on what other people think always puts you on shaky ground since it's only ever someone's opinion, and that can a) always change, and b) is outside of your control. When it comes to feeling calm, happy and good about yourself, doing things to impress or get approval from other people is a really bad idea. Don't get caught up in extrinsic goals – all those external things that society and other people tell you you should want. *Intrinsic* or internal goals are the real deal because they're just damn satisfying for *you*. Completing them, which doesn't depend on anyone else, is its own reward. Examples of intrinsic goals might be studying something because you find it totally fascinating, heading to the gym because you want to feel strong, or playing a musical instrument because it makes you feel free and soulful and you love seeing yourself improve. What intrinsic goals could you focus on?

. . . .

Self-esteem and busyness

Is being busy a badge of honour for you? Do you need constant work and activity in order to feel like you're worth something? Do you proudly proclaim how 'crazy busy' you are? The pressure is incredible and, yup, it's totally exhausting. Modern society may put worldly success and productivity up on a pedestal but, by now, it should be becoming obvious that permanent striving for them doesn't deliver results – at least not the ones we want. We run around, chase after goals, push to get things done, work hard and play harder for fear of missing out or 'not making the most of life'. Then we end up burnt out and too anxious to enjoy our lives.

Yes, it's good to set goals and work towards them, but not at the expense of your mental health. If you act like a Duracell bunny every hour of the day, then you're going to be an exhausted, anxious mess and that's no good for you or anyone else. You've got to recharge those batteries. Being constantly busy creates an overwhelming stream of information that your poor overworked brain has to process. You need breaks to work through it all. What's more, your adrenal glands, which are responsible for producing cortisol and adrenaline, need a rest from being constantly in 'go' mode. Can you start to view rest and relaxation as being just as 'productive' as busyness? Repeat after me: 'I need rest to be at my best.'

So if constant productivity and striving for success won't make us happy, what will? Perhaps it's having peace of mind, which is what helps us to feel good in the moment, right now. Or having great relationships and quality time with the people we love. Things totally changed for me when I set peace of mind as my priority; I became loads happier and calmer. I treat taking care of myself as my job, because it really is! I can't be a good person, therapist, writer, girlfriend or friend without first taking care of myself.

As the old saying goes, 'life is a journey' – but if you're too busy to enjoy it, what's the point? When your body is dead and gone, your achievements won't mean an awful lot. A lot of people love the saying, 'I'll sleep when I'm dead,' but that implies living life at breakneck speed, being 'on' all the time and potentially making yourself ill. The time to rest and enjoy yourself is now – don't underestimate its importance!

Self-care – the antidote to toxic busyness

When you're anxious and permanently on the go, self-care is often the last thing on your mind. It's a classic case of chicken and egg, because self-neglect can itself be a cause of anxiety. Either way, if you're feeling anxious or burnt out, then stepping up your self-care is an essential part of the solution. Looking after yourself sends you a powerful message that you matter, you're valuable and that you're worth taking care of. Maybe you won't believe it at first, but every time you do something kind and positive for yourself, even if it's as small as making sure your nails are always manicured and your eyebrows are neat and tidy, you reinforce the belief that you deserve it (and sweetheart, you absolutely do).

What would feel like self-care for you? Maybe you're a classic bubble-bath-and-glass-of-wine gal. Or maybe sitting in your favourite cafe doing nothing but watching the world go by puts you in the chill zone. Maybe it's borrowing the neighbour's dog and tramping round a field with, plus lots of doggy cuddles, that makes you feel really taken care of? Or maybe self-care means asking others for help and allowing yourself to receive it.

. . . .

Exercise: prioritize looking after yourself

Brainstorm at least twenty ideas that sum up self-care and relaxation for you. Schedule some of these into your diary and treat these appointments with the same importance you would a work meeting. When it's in the diary, it's set in stone. It might be having a walk at lunchtime, going for a yoga class or reading a book in the park for an hour. These are essential things, not a luxury.

Head to page 207 in The Anxiety Solution Toolkit in chapter nine to write down your twenty self-care ideas, then schedule some into the diary on page 208. If something is scheduled in, it's more likely to happen.

. . . .

Self-esteem and appearance

When I got to university, my brand-new student loan and sudden exposure to abundant cheap alcohol and fast food meant I quickly gained my 'fresher's 14' (lbs). But I soon started to worry about my weight and what I was eating. I believed I had to look like a Victoria's Secret model or a member of *The OC* in order to get a boyfriend and feel OK about myself. While I never had a full-blown eating disorder, I thought about food constantly and I rarely felt comfortable in my body, despite only being a UK size 12.

When we're unhappy with our bodies and the way we look, we're less likely to go out and enjoy our lives. We can become preoccupied with food and our weight, endlessly beating ourselves up about what we eat, which only adds another level of pressure and anxiety to our lives. Worries about how we look can become obsessive and may be a symptom of body dysmorphic disorder (BDD), which is a type of anxiety disorder. Always speak to your doctor or a therapist if you think you might have an eating disorder.

Eating disorders can be devastating, even fatal, but some level of disordered eating and anxiety around their bodies is a routine part of many women's lives. The YouGov 2015 Global Body Image Study found that 44 per cent of women are unhappy with their bodies.[1] Unsurprisingly, it's something that affects many more women than men.[2]

Research also suggests that anxiety about our bodies is more about the way we think than the reality of what we look like. Being super slim and beautiful doesn't stop you from having body anxiety, because the problem is generated by what's going on inside our brains, not by any objective 'truth'.

In her book *Rising Strong*, shame and vulnerability researcher Brené Brown tells us, 'Body image fear [is] the most common shame trigger for women.' It's the single biggest reason women don't feel good enough. 'Shame works like the zoom lens on a camera. When we are feeling shame, the camera is zoomed in tight and all we see is our flawed selves,' she writes. Brené's research has suggested that a whopping 90 per cent of women experience shame around body image. It's an almost universal trigger for not feeling good enough.

A study in 2003 by Dr Marika Tiggeman at Flinders University of South Australia, published in the *European Eating Disorders Review*, found that reading fashion and beauty magazines was linked to increased body dissatisfaction and rates of eating disorders.[3] That YouGov study also revealed that 74 per cent of us blame celebrity culture and social media for our body anxiety. Meanwhile, only about 5 per cent of us naturally have a body type comparable to the super-slim models we see on the TV and in magazines. It's like trying to fit a square peg into a (skinny) round hole. We're comparing ourselves to a body type that's just not what nature intended for most of us.

In 1995, TV was introduced to the island of Fiji (I know – how did they go so long without it!). Suddenly, young girls were being exposed to ads showing skinny American models and the glamorous lives of the characters on *Beverly Hills 90210*. Traditional Fijian culture had appreciated women with larger bodies but, following the introduction of television, girls on the island quickly became unhappy with their bodies. A study by psychiatrist Anne E. Becker revealed that 45 per cent of these girls showed signs of eating disorders and body anxiety, using purging methods such as laxatives and vomiting in order to lose weight.[4]

Try to view the media you consume as you do the food you eat. If you consume rubbish, you're going to feel that way. If you read a magazine or online gossip site that's fat-shaming some poor woman who's gained weight, or they've circled her cellulite with red pen, this is going to feed into your psyche about how it's wrong to be larger or have cellulite (which pretty much all women have anyway, even models – it's just airbrushed out!). If we read this sort of thing often enough it becomes a mental habit to be critical of ourselves and others and to find things like cellulite unacceptable.

Obviously, we can't avoid the media altogether, but curating what you watch and read can make all the difference. If a programme, magazine or website triggers a ton of self-doubt and worthlessness, ask yourself, is it worth reading/watching it? If following certain people on Instagram makes you hate your body, unfollow them. If watching *Made in Chelsea* makes you obsess over your muffin top, turn it off. It might only need to be a temporary measure, just until you feel more secure, but really, why expose yourself to things that make you feel like crap? For me, at certain times of the month or when I'm tired or having one of those days when I just don't feel great about myself, I'm especially careful about what I watch and listen to and I make sure I'm taking extra care of myself.

This issue really hit home to me when a client of mine told me that she spent dozens of anxious hours Googling and thinking about plastic surgery options. She was an incredibly attractive, slim, young woman, but that didn't mean a thing to her. In her mind, she wasn't good enough. The truth is it doesn't matter what you look like or how much you weigh, it's how you think about yourself that is important. In a world where 68 per cent of models suffer from anxiety or depression, we have to realize that having model good looks isn't any guarantee of happiness.[5]

Maybe you've told yourself, 'When I'm slimmer, finally I'll like myself and I can relax and be happy.' This is the wrong way round. Making peace with yourself first, the way you are, is the key to feeling attractive and confident, peaceful and happy. I found a lot of relief by giving myself permission to be who I was, and it can work for you, too. You don't need to be skinny or meet the definition of beauty determined by the fashion industry or celebrity culture. You just need to be you – that's enough. We can only ever feel good in the present moment. Can you give yourself permission right now to be OK with yourself as you are?

I recently went for a walk in Kew Gardens in London. It was looking completely gorgeous. The leaves on the trees were bursting with golden and orange shades; ducks and birds roamed free; mushrooms sprouted in the leaf mould. Nature was blooming in the carefree way that it does. The gnarly branches of a tree don't much care about what you think of them. They don't compare themselves to other trees. The mushrooms don't fret about their irregular, knobbly shape. Birds don't worry about the tunefulness of their singing.

Nature just expresses itself. It is what it is, and it's beautiful, in all its imperfections. And guess what? You're a part of nature, too! Try to recognize this and to realize that you're fine just as you are.

Whenever I notice myself becoming critical about my body I come back to this idea that I'm a part of nature. In the same way that I don't judge a cat for being too hairy, or a dog for having a wet nose, I won't judge myself for having thighs that wobble when I walk or hair that won't stay straight in the rain. The majority of our criticisms are about how we look compared to someone else or how we think we *should* look. But Mother Nature didn't make any mistakes when she made you; you're exactly how you should be. And if reaching a healthy weight is a goal for you, accepting and loving yourself, as you are, is always the most motivating way to get there. Love wins over hate every time.

If you think I'm over-stressing the role confidence and self-love can play in your sense of your own attractiveness, try this. Imagine two twins of equal physical attractiveness. One is having fun and looking confident and relaxed. The other is self-conscious, hunched over and worried-looking. No prize for guessing which one appears more attractive. Confidence is one of the most attractive qualities you can possess. And unlike your breasts, it's easy to increase it without having to resort to drastic (surgical) measures. Instead of worrying about how you look, focus on feeling confident and good about yourself instead. There are loads of ideas and inspiration for doing this in the Anxiety Solution Toolkit in Chapter nine but here's one very powerful exercise to get you started.

. . . .

Exercise: boost your body confidence

In her book *Life Loves You*, author Louise Hay describes a technique called mirror work, which enables you to change your perception of yourself. You stand in front of a mirror and look into your own eyes as you tell yourself the positive things you want to take on board. You could say things such as, 'I am enough, I love myself, I am an attractive and confident person.' There's something very powerful and meaningful about looking into your own eyes and saying it out loud to yourself – just make sure your housemate is out while you do it. (Unless she wants to get in on it, too!) You'll find, with enough repetition, that you begin to believe it.

. . . .

Self-esteem and inner talk

It had been a hectic day and my brain was fried. I'd been sitting at my computer for hours agonizing over a tech issue, but now I had to go to a networking event. As I walked into the busy room, I spotted someone I knew and made my way over. I was tired and not feeling myself and I tried to make a joke that just didn't land. I got con-fused and it came out all wrong. I felt my face getting hot and a horrible wave of shame and self-judgement come crashing over me. My internal dialogue turned nasty. '*Ugh! Why am I such an idiot! She's not going to want to talk to me again! Why can't I just be normal?*'

At this point, I had a choice: to carry on beating myself up and end up feeling even crappier, or to put it through the friend filter. So I put myself in my best friend's shoes. What would she say about this? As soon as I had this thought, I could already hear her laughing it off. 'It's not a big deal, she probably didn't even notice! Chloe, you're great, all your friends love you. You were just tired. Tomorrow, this won't matter. And who wants to be nor-mal anyway!?' I felt better almost instantly.

When I first ask my clients how they speak to them-selves, they'll often stare at me blankly. It's not something many of us think about. But we are always talking to ourselves in our heads. 'You look so fat today. No one really likes you. You never do anything right. You're a fucking loser, you may as well give up.' On and on goes the negative chatter. It's not nice, is it? Would you talk to your bestie that way? I bet not – and if you did, you'd better believe she'd ditch you pretty quick! This is the way many of us talk to ourselves all the time. Often we're not even aware of it; it just happens on autopilot, but it's high time you became aware, because being a bully has never helped anyone.

You're not alone – pretty much every single one of us

carries these critical voices around with us in our heads. But here's the thing. They aren't telling the truth. Honest. It can be really hard to remember that, though, so when those thoughts are plaguing you, try to see things from the perspective of someone who loves you. And it might sound odd, but that mean inner voice is actually *trying* to help you learn something from the situation so you don't do it again. (True, its technique sucks – but its instinct is to keep you safe.)

Many of us subconsciously believe that we need to be hard on ourselves in order to get better. We think that if we're too nice to ourselves we'll slack off and nothing will get done! But as anyone who had critical parents or a critical teacher will know, criticism only makes you feel bad about yourself, and that's hardly inspiring or motivating. In fact, there's plenty of evidence to suggest that being overly self-critical can be linked to our upbringing.[6] If you had critical parents or a dysfunctional or insecure family upbringing, you're more likely to give yourself a hard time. While you can't change the past, there *is* good news! Being self-critical is a learnt behaviour, which means you can unlearn it and create a new, kinder way of being.

In her book *Self-Compassion: Stop Beating Yourself Up and Leave Insecurity Behind,* Dr Kristin Neff, associate professor of human development at the University of Texas, Austin, demonstrates that people who are kind and supportive towards themselves are more motivated to do better than those who have a harsh inner dialogue. So if you think giving yourself hell over little mistakes is going to help, you're dead wrong. When we're hard on ourselves it makes us more afraid of failure, and when we fear failure we're less likely to even try. Being kind isn't about lowering your standards. It's a way of encouraging and supporting yourself to be the best you can be. We are all imperfect; we all make mistakes. None of us escapes fucking things up sometimes. Self-compassion is about being OK with our imperfections rather than judging and criticizing ourselves. We all need and deserve that.

. . . .

Exercise: kind? Or kind of a bitch?

It's time to get honest with yourself about your self-talk. Are you being kind? Or kind of a bitch? I recommend checking in with yourself several times a day – set a reminder on your phone or calendar – to ask yourself, 'How am I speaking to myself now?' Make a note of what you discover. If it's not very nice, then you could try one of my favourite techniques for silencing my inner Mean Girl, which is to turn her into a character with a silly voice. It could be Donald Duck or Mickey Mouse or Angelica Pickles, the meanie from *The Rugrats*! Mine is Toad (of Toad Hall) dressed as a washerwoman, with a really high-pitched voice (this is random, but it works for me!), and when I hear her telling me that I'm useless or that I'm not good enough, I just tell her to pipe down and be quiet! By seeing your inner critic as a character with a silly voice, you can start to take it less seriously and recognize that it's not the real you, that it's not helpful and that you can safely ignore it.

Another powerful tool is to put all that mean talk through the friend filter: would you speak to a friend like that? Would *your* best friend speak to you like that? If the answer is 'no', it's time to make a change. How can you change your self-talk so that it's kinder, more positive and supportive? Make a note of how you would speak to yourself having 'friend filtered' it. Write out a different script for your self-talk. As you repeat this exercise it will become more and more automatic to speak to yourself in a kind and loving way.

· ·

Self-esteem and people-pleasing

If you constantly worry about what other people think of you, you're setting yourself up for misery. Actually, it's none of *your* business what others think about you. Their opinions are just that: only an opinion, and besides, they always speak more about themselves than they do about you.

Most of us believe that our opinions (and those of other people) are in some way true. We think the way we see the world is like a video camera, taking in everything and perceiving it as it really is. But this isn't true. We are actually more like projectors, beaming out our thoughts, beliefs and experiences on to the world and, in the process, creating what we see. When another person sees you, they're not seeing the *real you*. They're seeing all their own beliefs, experiences and emotions – and projecting them on to you. And you can't control any of that! Their upbringing, beliefs about how people 'should' act, the sort of day they've had or whether you remind them of someone else can all come into play. This doesn't mean you should never take on board any feedback from other people. It just means that you should avoid taking on that heavy responsibility for what other people think of you. There's a lot of relief to be gained from admitting it's OK not to be liked by everyone.

Many of us take on far too much responsibility for what other people think and feel. When we're children we learn that other people's feelings are our responsibility. Growing up, I felt that, if Mum was upset or angry, it was my fault and my job to fix it. If Dad was irritable or worried, I would feel horribly guilty. I was a sensitive child! But children don't understand that other people's own pain and hurt is the main cause of their negative feelings.

We want people to like us and we may even try to change ourselves so that they do. The problem is, thinking we can control another person's thoughts and feelings is delusional. People think and feel the way they do because of their own stuff. Yes, we should do our best to take on board other people's feelings, be considerate, helpful and supportive, but it's vital that we recognize that there are limits to what we can or should do, especially if it means we are squashing parts of ourselves. Most people with anxiety take on board way too much responsibility for other people's issues. Trying to mould yourself or supressing your true self in order to please others is hugely stressful and a sure-fire way to stay anxious.

Self-esteem and 'comparisonitis'

It might only take a glimpse at your Instagram feed to trigger an internal dialogue along the lines of, 'Why am I not doing more with my life? I should be cooking exquisite yet healthy and artfully arranged food every day! Why is everyone out having so much fun while I sit here feeling crap? I shouldn't have eaten that bowl of pasta . . . maybe that's why I have so much flesh on my inner thighs . . .' Blah blah blah.

When we compare our lives with other people's, it's easy for worries about how we 'must do and be better' to spiral into full-on self-loathing. But remember, these people are not posting about the #periodpain #bloating #anxious-as-all-hell and #self-loathing that a lot of them are feeling, even those with the supposedly perfect lives. That's because, well, it probably wouldn't sell stuff or get as many likes. But I guarantee that everyone, no matter how great their lives may appear online, has something shitty going on. Everyone is dealing with something and no one is giving us the whole story on their social media feed.

Back in the fifties, psychologist Leon Festinger devised the social comparison theory. It states that humans have an inbuilt desire to evaluate how they're doing. We'll often use comparison as a way to do this. The problem is that, nowadays, comparison has got totally out of control because we're comparing ourselves not just to Katie who lives down the road but to Taylor Swift, Karlie Kloss and unlimited other superstars and models. The fact that we're so exposed, 24/7, to the world's richest, most successful and beautiful people means we're comparing ourselves to standards that are unattainable for 99 per cent of the population. (Saying that, even if you *are* one of the 1 per cent you're not immune to comparison because there's always someone younger, richer and more beautiful living a more 'fun' life than you. There are no winners in the comparison game.)

But even comparing ourselves to our peers can be really toxic. If your Facebook feed is anything like mine, it's flooded with pictures of school friends in white dresses and/or with their adorable babies. We see everyone's gorgeous holiday selfies, their blossoming careers and the number of likes they have on their posts. It's great to see our friends doing well but it can also create a huge amount of pressure and a desperate sense that we're being left behind. We end up focusing on what we don't have or haven't (yet) achieved, and it's all too easy to decide there's something wrong with us.

This is when it's crucial to come back to our own lives. Firstly, remember to ask yourself whether you really do want those things (whether it's marriage or babies or a high-flying career) or whether they're the things society says you *ought* to want. It's also really helpful to appreciate all the amazing things we *do* have. And, above all, remember that there will always be people who are more successful/attractive/smart/interesting/whatever than you are. That's just a fact of life. If you're constantly comparing yourself to others, nothing good can come of it. It's a battle you can't win and an addiction you need to give up. So I'm declaring here and now that 'I'm out!' of the comparison party and I invite you to join me.

Connection rather than competition

If you're comparing yourself to someone, why not reach out and congratulate them instead? If that's not possible, mentally cheer them on. Celebrate the accomplishments of other people and your own. Pile praise on your colleague who just got promoted. Wish your friend well on her round-the-world trip. The energy of support and connection is so much better than that of comparison and competition. Your anxiety will decrease and you'll feel better.

Allow yourself to be inspired by the other person. Maybe their achievements and successes can ignite a passion to take some positive action for yourself? When other people do well, it shows us what's possible.

Sometimes, when we're comparing ourselves with others, it's because there's a part of us that knows that we're capable of doing or achieving what the other person has. So if you really want something, whether it's to buy a house or a Burberry coat, have a child or a great career, trust that it's on the way to you or make a plan to make it happen. Otherwise, let it go and focus on what's going great for you right now.

I used to put myself down and compare myself to other women doing similar work to me. These days I get inspired by others, by the exciting opportunities available and about what's possible. I mentally cheer them on rather than beating myself up for not being the same as them. Then I focus fully on the fantastic things that are happening in my world and appreciate myself for all the progress I've made and how far I've come. You can do the same.

Just do *you*

There isn't, nor will there ever be, another you. You are a one-time event in the universe. You have your own unique blend of gifts and strengths *and* your own unique challenges and struggles. It's time to celebrate yourself and to acknowledge that everyone is special in his or her own way. No one can do things quite the way you do; no one has the personality, sense of humour, quirks or style you have.

You are not here to be better at things than other people; you're here to be the best that you can possibly be. If you're going to compare yourself to anyone, let it be to yourself. You are always growing and learning. That's a damn certainty. There are things that you can do today that you wouldn't have been able to do five or ten years ago. You've overcome difficulties, gained insights, evolved as a person. You've helped other people along the way, too. Remind yourself of all the progress you've made and that you continue to make. You're amazing!

· ·

Exercise: cure your 'comparisonitis'

Keep a gratitude journal, or 'jar of awesome'. (See page 181 for the jar of awesome and check out the Anxiety Solution Toolkit in Chapter nine for lots of ideas on how to bring about a sense of calm gratitude for what you already have.) It can also help to do a media cleanse and, if you need to, un-follow anyone who triggers unhelpful comparisons. Focus on yourself and all the progress you've made. Make a list of all the things you've learnt, all the insights you've gained, the people you've helped and the success you've had. Recognize the way you've grown as a person over the years, even through your struggles. Focus on being the best that *you* can be. Finally, support and cheer on other women who are doing well. Connect rather than compete. Use them as inspiration to fuel your own success.

· ·

Summary

★ Feeling that nothing we do is good enough and that we must be perfect in order to be loved is practically a universal anxiety.

★ The antidote to this perfectionism is healthy and realistic self-esteem.

★ Healthy self-esteem doesn't mean being an egotistical monster. It means believing that you are an intrinsically valuable person, just as you are, and being as kind to yourself as you would be to a friend.

★ When we have healthy self-esteem we stop worrying what other people think of us, stop comparing ourselves to others and focus on our own goals and pleasures.

CHAPTER 5

Decisions, decisions

Sometimes you make the right decision,
sometimes you make the decision right.
DR PHIL MCGRAW

Does making decisions leave you anxious and overwhelmed? You're not alone. We all have to make
decisions all day long, from little things, such as what
to wear, which email to reply to first and what to eat for
dinner to bigger ones such as – you know – where to
live, what to do for a job and what to do with our lives
(eek!). We've never had so many decisions to make. One
of the advantages of the modern world is that it's made
so many possibilities available to us, but the downside
is it can all feel overwhelming. So much so that we end
up shying away from choosing for fear of making the
'wrong' choice. Everyone gets overwhelmed sometimes
but if you suffer from anxiety you are more prone to
beating yourself up about your past decisions, convinced you made bad ones. When we're anxious, even
stuff that's pretty unimportant in the big scheme of
things – which brand of butter or dog food to buy in

the supermarket – can seem impossible to resolve. Sometimes we end up in analysis paralysis, taking no action at all because it's all too scary.

Spoilt by choice

Can you have too much of a good thing? Apparently so. Having too much choice seems like a First World problem (and it is), but it's no less real for that. We're drowning in options, and it's stressing us out.

My client Katherine, forty-two, tells me, 'I find it hard to concentrate in the supermarket. I get so distracted. I always used to plan meals for the week as I walked around but I just can't manage it any more. These days, I have to do online shops, with my spreadsheet open.'

Barry Schwartz, author of *The Paradox of Choice*, carried out a study that showed that when confronted with twenty-four flavours of jam, participants were *less* likely to buy one than if there were only six flavours. The over-abundance of choice makes it harder to decide, so would-be buyers end up purchasing nothing. Having more options can mean you're unable to make decisions because it's just so damn confusing.

Too many choices can also lead to you thinking that the elusive 'perfect' option must exist, if only you could figure it out. Whether it's finding your perfect pair of jeans (I've been there; the search continues), planning the best possible holiday or choosing your ideal partner on

Tinder, having infinite choices and endless information at your fingertips means you can set your standards incredibly high and put pressure on yourself not to make a 'bad' decision.

Schwartz's research suggests that analysing and agonizing over every possibility is making us miserable and that those who are able to settle for 'good enough' are far more likely to find contentment. Searching for perfection is kind of like chasing a unicorn: you'll never find it and you'll end up exhausted and dispirited in the process. If you're prone to perfectionism, ask yourself, 'Is this decision good enough?' Good enough *is* good enough! Make it and move on.

Suffering from decision fatigue

There's a reason we get so worn out by decision-making: it literally uses up mental energy. The process of choosing drains our willpower, which, according to the American Psychological Association, is a finite resource.[1] It also uses up glucose, because your brain runs on sugar, so don't be surprised if you're constantly reaching for the chocolate bars or sweets when you're trying to choose, decide or make plans. Basically, making decisions is hard work and if your anxious mind is causing you to analyse every single tiny choice, you're going to end up exhausted pretty quickly. (Reportedly, Barack Obama and Mark Zuckerberg wear the same thing every day – a suit and a grey T-shirt, respectively – to take that one decision-making process out of their lives, freeing up mental energy for bigger, more important decisions.) If you think decision fatigue may be wearing you out, have a look at your life to see whether you could eradicate some areas of decision-making. (I mean, if it works for Obama and Zuckerberg, it must be good.)

Having a solid routine can help you create structure, which removes the need for decision-making and feels comforting. For example, I like having the same morning routine each day. I also like exercising at the same time, having fewer options in my wardrobe and sticking to a shopping list when I buy food.

Decluttering and having a more minimal, streamlined home can also save you mental energy. All those annoying little things – the key for the filing cabinet you can't find, the cupboard stuffed with empty boxes you need to throw out, the kitchen drawer that's a mess – all subtly drain you of energy. I recently decluttered a load of my clothes and beauty products. I now have fewer options and each choice is a no-brainer. Simpler equals better in my view.

There are no perfect decisions

My client Carley, twenty-six, from Hertfordshire, blames her perfectionism and overly high expectations on decision-making anxiety. 'I had this huge anxiety about whether to go travelling. I was trying to decide whether to buy a European train pass, worrying about things like whether it would be worth the money or not. I wanted to have the "perfect" summer but I wound myself into such a state wondering if it was the "right" decision or not. I spiralled into a deeply anxious state because of it.'

Reminder: there are no 'perfect' decisions. It's all about your attitude. Things can feel perfect when you accept them as they are and accept that your best is good enough. Once you've made a decision, what you make of the outcome is key. Your anxious mind can trick you into thinking things are black and white and that decisions are either good or bad. But that's not the way it works. If you really can't decide between two things, could it be that both are good choices? Pushing to try to make things perfect often makes you miserable. There are numerous good possibilities out there for you and there is no single solution to any problem.

Plus, external factors outside of your control can change outcomes. You choose to go on holiday to France, for example, but it rains for a few days so you can't do all the things you'd hoped to do. Was there an error in your decision-making? Nope, it's just a shame that it rained. You made the right decision for you at the time. Nothing in life stays the same; everything is changing constantly. We can't always control what happens, but we can control how we respond to events. Learning to recognize what's outside of your control can mean the difference between anxiety and calm.

An obsession with the perfect decision often stems from a fear of making a mistake. But mistakes are an inevitable part of life, so to expect yourself never to make any is just plain unfair! Besides, without them you wouldn't have any opportunities for learning. I wonder how many so-called 'mistakes' have led you to opportunities you never would have had otherwise? You choose to walk to the station instead of getting the bus and end up missing the train but it leads to an incredible conversation with someone you meet on the platform. You get lost, but you discover a new part of town you haven't been to before. You go out with a guy who turns out to be a dick, but you rediscover how much you love your friends in the process. Never underestimate how much a supposedly bad decision can end up helping you. Every experience has something to teach you, as long as you're open to it.

Sometimes, when I'm struggling, I pretend I'm the lovable lead in an eighties movie during the 'training montage' – you know, those sections where the character is shown struggling, failing and trying over and over again to accomplish something, all to a cheesy soundtrack. The best example is probably that bit in *Dirty Dancing* where Baby is learning to dance with Johnny. She starts out being rubbish but by the end of the song, and the montage of shots, she has mastered most of the moves and is on her way to being a dancing star (and being in love with Patrick Swayze's character). Your life is like that training montage. Trying things, learning a lot and finally triumphing, but not before a lot of mistakes and failures, is what we all have to go through. Even when you fail, the audience – your friends, your family, Mother Nature, the universe! – is rooting for you and knows you'll succeed eventually. Keep going, because you are always learning and making progress. And remember that the people who really matter will love you, no matter what.

You choose your outcome

Michael Neill, life coach and author of *The Inside Out Revolution*, says any decision is far less important than how you deal with whatever arises from it. You can *make* your decisions good. You can handle and adapt to whatever results from that choice.

I used to get caught up in little decisions, such as which restaurant to suggest for a night out with a friend. I would spend the whole time worrying about whether they liked it and whether I'd made the 'right' choice, so much so that it was hard for me to just relax and enjoy the evening. Now I tell myself that it's up to me to make the decision good by accepting it and focusing on enjoying it as much as possible.

You can make almost any decision the 'right' one by adjusting the attitude you bring to it. Be kind to yourself about the decisions you make. Notice the way you speak to yourself about your choices and apply the friend filter: would you speak to your best friend like that if she were worrying about a decision? Try saying a daily affirmation to yourself, such as, 'I trust myself to make decisions' or 'I am capable and wise.' One of my favourites is 'I make the best of every decision.'

Remember, very few decisions are final. Most of the time, life is a series of adjustments. If you weren't keen on what you chose for dinner, you can make something else tomorrow. If you don't like the holiday destination, you go somewhere else next time. If you move in with your partner and they turn out *not* to be The One, you can move out again. Yes, that would be rubbish, but maybe you wouldn't know until you tried. There is almost always a way to reverse decisions if they really don't work out.

Get ready to leap

Overthinking decisions is a classic way of trying to control the outcomes. When we're anxious, we hate uncertainty. We need assurance that things will work out. We overthink things in order to try to control every variable and, sometimes, it makes us feel safer. But how often do events turn out exactly as we planned? Hardly ever – there are simply too many variables and things outside of our control. When it comes to making decisions, *no* amount of analysis can take all the risk out of it. It might seem easier not to make a decision at all because, that way, at least things will stay the same. It feels safer to stick with what you know. But each time you do that you miss an opportunity for growth.

Life is an experiment, and there's no rule book. Even super-confident people will admit that, some of the time, they're making it up as they go along. Remind yourself that you've had a wealth of valuable experiences and that you are equipped with everything you need to make good decisions.

Besides, the only way to truly know the outcome of a decision is to take the leap and go for it. Scary, but true. No amount of thinking can replace experience. No amount of worrying can give you the clarity that taking action will. You're never going to really know what it will be like to live in another city until you try it. You won't know how your business idea will be received until you start it. Taking the safe option can keep you stuck and hold you back. That worst-case scenario you keep replaying in your mind? It's hugely unlikely. A possibility and a probability are not the same thing. Try to remember that, if your brain is telling you something is too risky, it could just be the anxiety talking.

When you take action, you learn to trust yourself because you prove to yourself that you can always handle whatever arises. You'll handle it because you're a smart, adaptable and creative human being who has resources and strengths that you're able to call upon when you need them. If you quit your job to become self-employed and it doesn't work out, for example, then yes, it's a bit shit, but you can always go and get another job. When you take a leap, you adjust and adapt to make the best of the decision you've made. If you're still not sure, start with a small step and test the water. Often, anxiety recedes once you take action and realize that it's not as dangerous as you thought.

At a workshop I was running I met a woman called Maddie. She said that no matter what happens she tells herself, 'This is what's supposed to happen.' Whether she believed in fate or believed that life had a plan, I'm not sure. But having this attitude helped her to meet every situation with the acceptance that things were unfolding as they should and she could make the best of every situation. If a decision didn't turn out as she'd hoped, she just told herself, 'This is what's meant to happen' and adapted to it. It's about accepting reality rather than arguing with it and wishing things were different. So, if you end up running late because you took a different route to work or having dinner in a crappy restaurant that you chose, hey, it was meant to happen! Don't beat yourself up. Everything is happening perfectly.

Avoid making decisions when you're anxious or tired

If you've ever suspected that anxiety means it's harder for your brain to make decisions, you're right. A study published in the *Journal of Neuroscience* in 2016 found that anxiety disrupts the prefrontal cortex, making it harder to take rational decisions or weigh up plans for the future.[2]

The amygdala – the fear centre of the brain – takes the wheel and insists it would be better to play it safe. The study, done on rats, found that when they were anxious they were more likely to become distracted and therefore make poorer decisions. And it makes sense: when we're anxious, negative thoughts, worries and physical sensations can distract us from focusing in the moment. Being more mindful and present is the antidote to distractions getting in the way of our decision-making.

When you're anxious, you're also more likely to think about your dilemmas in black and white terms. It's all or nothing, either good or bad, safe or dangerous. There's no middle ground. This isn't rational and it can lead to your making poor decisions or prevent you from choosing things that could be great opportunities. Overthinking rarely leads to anything good. Creative insights don't arise from mind-numbing worry and over-analysing everything until it no longer makes sense. More thinking doesn't always mean better thinking. It often just makes things confusing rather than clearer.

Taking yourself away from the situation and giving yourself permission *not* to think about it can sometimes create the space you need to think clearly. For maximum clarity and more inspired decisions, breaks are essential; even better if you can take them outdoors (or at least away from your desk). Archimedes had his eureka moment while chilling in the bath. Sir Isaac Newton was having a rest under a tree when the apple fell on his head and he came up with his theory of gravity.

Evidence suggests that the beginning of the day is the best time for making big or important decisions. This is when most people's mental-energy resources are at their highest. Don't make decisions when you're tired or extremely anxious because your brain won't be at its best and you're more likely to be irrational. Taking the pressure off yourself and taking time to relax are very important.

Trust your gut

Sometimes your first thought or gut reaction is the best one. Here's what Malcolm Gladwell, author of *Blink: The Power of Thinking Without Thinking*, has to say about making decisions.

> We live in a world that assumes that the quality of a decision is directly related to the time and effort that went into making it . . . We believe that we are always better off gathering as much information as possible and spending as much time as possible in deliberation. We really only trust conscious decision-making. But there are moments when our snap judgements and first impressions can offer a much better means of making sense of the world. The first task of *Blink* is to convince you of a simple fact: decisions made very quickly can be every bit as good as decisions made cautiously and deliberately.

Learning to listen to and trust your gut or your intuition, or whatever you want to call it, may be the key to making decisions more easily. But the trouble with trusting your gut is that it's easy to confuse gut feelings with fear. We all know our guts react to our emotions (nervous tummy, anyone?) so how can we tell whether it's the anxiety talking or our intuition?

Most of us are out of touch with our intuition; we're so tuned into the mental noise in our brains that we can't hear the calm, wise, quiet voice inside us. Intuition tends to be a gentle inkling, while fear screams and shouts. Intuition is unemotional and affirming, while fear is emotional and demeaning.

It's not fully known how gut feelings are generated, but it has been suggested that, rather than some mystical sixth sense, they represent the wisdom we gain from our experiences, one that goes beyond the conscious mind to the subconscious. It's certainly true that the gut contains millions of nerve cells and is often referred to as the 'second brain', which could explain things.

Wherever these insights come from, something interesting happens with decision-making when we relax about it. When we calm our minds and let go of trying to control the outcome, we're more able to tap into our inner wisdom, our intuition and our deeper understanding.

Exercise: **talking to your gut**

Here are some questions to ask yourself that will help you to distinguish gut feelings from fear. Try answering them out loud to yourself or writing down ideas in your notebook. Ideally, do it out in nature or at a time when you're more relaxed. Tune into your body and ask yourself, Do I feel good about this decision? Which of these options 'feels' right to me?

Does the thought of taking this decision give me energy or drain my energy?

Is it possible that the fear I feel about this decision is really excitement? Am I catastrophizing? Is the worst-case scenario really that bad? Is it even likely? What would a friend say about this? Is this something I am often anxious or fearful about?

Now try this technique from Michael Neill. Assign two things you're trying to decide between to the two sides of a coin. Now, flip the coin. (Try it right now if you have something you're deliberating over!) Flipped your coin? How do you feel about the result? Whether you're pleased or disappointed could indicate what the best decision for you might really be. If you're ambivalent, it could be a sign that it doesn't really matter and that either will be good for you.

Don't get scared, get excited

When I first started public speaking I was absolutely bloody terrified! Beyond nervous. It took on a nightmarish quality. Dread would hang over me for weeks before having to speak. I remember having this huge sense of confusion about whether speaking up and 'putting myself out there' was the 'right' thing. Was my gut warning me that public speaking just wasn't for me? Every cell in my body was telling me to avoid it. Was it a 'sign' that I wasn't ready? Or was it just fear and anxiety taking over, clouding my judgement?

Fear holds lots of us back. That makes sense, because it feels so real, though it almost always isn't. My fear of speaking in public was so overwhelming that for a long time I believed it. But something deeper inside me was saying 'yes'. It was just a whisper at first, but I couldn't shake the feeling that I was meant to overcome this fear, not continue to let it beat me.

A couple of years ago I went to a personal development workshop with a woman called Katrina Love Senn. I talked to her about my fear of speaking in public. I remember her telling me, 'It's all about how you look at it. What if you stopped seeing it as a nightmare and instead saw it as an adventure?'

That was a turning point for me. I decided I had to view the things I was scared to do as exciting rather than frightening. After all, many of the 'symptoms' of fear are the same as those of excitement: butterflies, increased heart rate and the release of adrenaline. 'Fear is excitement without breath,' said Robert Heller, author of *Achieving Excellence*. I didn't change in an instant and it's something I still have to work on but I now choose to label any nervous feelings or anxiety as excitement rather than fear.

In 2013 Alison Brooks, a professor at Harvard Business School, coined the term 'anxious reappraisal'. Her study found that saying 'I feel excited' before a performance is more helpful than trying to calm yourself down. This is because anxiety and excitement are so closely linked in terms of how they feel and *reframing* the physical sensations is easier to do than trying to control them.[3]

Can you start to relabel fearful, nervous or anxious feelings as excitement? Is the fear you feel about going travelling, leaving your job, starting a business or speaking up really excitement about what possibilities lie ahead? Is that feeling of dread really a call to adventure? Try repeating a mantra such as 'I feel excited about my decisions.'

Forgo the people-pleasing

I was recently chatting to my friend Maria about planning a holiday. Although she's ordinarily one of the calmest people I know, there's one thing that can turn her into a ball of worry, even to the point of having sleepless nights. Maria gets paralysed with indecision, especially when her decision-making involves other people. She wants things to be perfect and feels the need to please everyone so they all have the best time ever. She was convinced that if, God forbid, the holiday didn't measure up, she would be to blame. Juggling everyone else's feelings had created a huge amount of stress and anxiety and made it really hard for her to move forward with a plan, for fear of 'getting it wrong'. She confessed that she couldn't even figure out what *she* wanted, among all the mental noise. What should have been a fun experience had turned into an angst-ridden ordeal. It was getting too late to book anything and she was worried it wouldn't end up happening at all.

As a considerate person, you probably want to avoid upsetting people if you can. Perhaps, though, you take this a bit too far and try to keep everyone happy all of the time, even if, deep down, you know you're doomed to fail because it simply isn't possible. If you keep trying, your own happiness and peace of mind will suffer. You could end up burning out. This is another case where learning to accept 'good enough' is vital. Doing your best for others but ultimately doing what you want and what you know to be best for you is the only sustainable way to live. Ask yourself, are you taking on board too much responsibility for other people's happiness? Are you losing sight of what you want and pushing yourself too hard on others' behalf? If you struggle with feeling selfish when you put yourself first, remember this: when you take care of yourself, it ends up benefiting others because you're more fulfilled and energized and have more to give.

Fight back against procrastination

Anxiety and procrastination are inextricably linked in a classic chicken-and-egg situation. Procrastination causes anxiety and anxiety causes procrastination. Who hasn't occasionally found themselves hooked on *Game of Thrones* or make-up tutorials on YouTube when they should be working, studying or doing life admin? But if procrastination is getting in the way of you achieving your heart's desires, getting good results in your work or studies or, worse, actually *causing* more anxiety, then it's time to address it.

I know the feeling of procrastinating all too well – that sweet relief of deciding to 'do it tomorrow'. It's a temporary freedom from having to do something difficult, boring or scary. I very often used to start a day with big plans and goals, only to end it with a sparkling clean house, a jumpin' Facebook page and an unfinished to-do list. This would be followed by horrible feelings of worthlessness, guilt, frustration and anguish over all the things I should have been doing.

Studies have linked procrastination with low self-belief, low self-esteem[4] and fear – ironically, fear of either failure *or* success. If we're pressuring ourselves to make perfect decisions and we're terrified of failure, then it can feel a whole lot easier to put things off or to dump our dreams and goals completely so that we never let ourselves down. We convince ourselves we don't really want what we want, or that it's just not worth the effort or risk. We make excuses about 'not being ready' or 'not being good enough'. We tell ourselves we're not an expert so we can't possibly give that talk, or we're not thin enough to start going on dates or fit enough to begin yoga. But everyone has to start somewhere and you're almost guaranteed to get better at it, whatever it is, once you actually get started. Entrepreneur Richard Branson advises starting something *before* you're ready. You just need to begin and then trust that you *will* get better as you go along.

A couple of years ago I was on the brink of taking some big (think *scary*) steps in my career, but I kept putting them off. I was letting a constant stream of *busyness* get in the way of the things I really wanted to do. I was allowing fear to hold me back. 'What if I'm laughed at? What if I get it wrong? What if everyone hates me?!' I had a strong fear of failure, but I actually feared success even more. 'What happens if it goes well but I can't sustain the success, or it's too much hard work and I end up worn out and miserable?'

Recognizing our fears is the first step towards overcoming them. I started to see mine for what they were, called them out and made a decision to move forward with my plans anyway. I told myself I could cross the bridge of how to sustain my success when I came to it.

So I began to take small steps. I tackled my priority tasks first thing in the morning, when my mojo is at its highest. Progress didn't happen overnight but I'm happy to say I've moved forward with my plans and I'm able to speak in public, go to networking events and work the room and run my online program – all things I didn't think I'd be able to do in the past.

Remember, there is no shame in failing. Ask any successful person and they'll tell you all about the numerous failures they've had. It's all a natural part of the process of learning and growing. Don't let trying to be perfect get in the way of being good.

Can you identify what fears could be causing you to procrastinate? Below are some actionable things for you to try when procrastination is holding you back.

Eat that frog

Mmmm, frog – everyone's favourite, right?! It's tempting to want to start the day with a few easy tasks to ease yourself in gently. You know the drill. Pop off a few casual emails; organize your stationery drawer; check in on how the Kardashians are doing; make four cups of tea. But this is a big mistake. Huge! Productivity guru Brian Tracy says that, actually, we need to 'eat that frog'. By this he means eating (doing) the ugliest frog (most difficult/ annoying task) before you do anything else. Committing to doing the hardest task first takes the decision-making out of it. You super-charge your self-esteem because, yay, you've done something hard and it's only 10 a.m.! This sets a strong precedent for the day. Winning at a difficult task early on increases your momentum, motivation and confidence and inspires you to get on with other tricky stuff, too. So rather than starting your day with a leisurely snoop around social media and some low-level emails that could really wait (or be deleted?!), begin by making that difficult phone call or tackling the nightmare spreadsheet. It will transform your mood and is a bullet-proof procrastination buster.

Tim Ferriss, lifestyle guru and author of *The 4-Hour Workweek: Escape 9–5, Live Anywhere and Join the New Rich,* suggests you also commit to doing the simple task of making your bed every morning. This small achievement can lead to bigger achievements throughout the day.

Don't waste time online

Social media and emails can rob you of a lot of time. As we've already seen, they can also cause anxiety – so that's another reason to limit your exposure. If I don't keep myself in check, I can cruise social media or emails several times *an hour*. It's too easy to get lost down the rabbit hole of celebrity gossip or in stalking the holiday snaps of your colleague from seven years ago. In addition to the obvious time wasted, each time we do this it takes a while to get back on task. Deadline anxiety, anyone?

There's a reason Instagram is so addictive. For our brains, checking social media is akin to taking a pleasure-enhancing drug. In his book *Focus: The Hidden Driver of Excellence*, Daniel Goleman explains that checking emails and Facebook sets off a reward mechanism similar to the one triggered by taking cocaine. That's right – your little 'hit' of information, whether it's Kardashian gossip or a sensational news story, is getting you hooked. You can tackle this by turning off the Wi-Fi on your computer while you work, preventing notifications from being pushed to your phone or using an app like Anti-Social (antisocial.80pct.com) to block distracting websites between certain times.

Take little steps

When the things we're trying to do just seem too damn big and scary, procrastination is particularly hard to resist. David Allen, author of *Getting Things Done: The Art of Stress-free Productivity*, suggests that rather than trying to do too much at once it's better to break tasks down into teeny-tiny steps and just do one small thing at a time. Setting a time limit for each stage also helps you focus and become more productive, because if a task has no time limits it can feel overwhelming and may never get done. For example, if you want to take up running, break this goal down into all the things you need to do to get you out there. It might be spending half an hour research-ing running clubs near you or buying some new trainers and then going out for your first twenty-minute jog. Small steps add up to big ones, and you'll grow your confidence and self-belief in the process.

Schedule everything in

I put things off a lot less when I schedule my day by the hour. A surprising amount of time can be wasted trying to decide what task to do next, or just by taking too many cheeky little breaks. When I schedule every single thing on my to-do list, I know exactly what I'm doing and when. I also schedule breaks. That way I don't miss out on the rest I need but I don't end up wasting time making a cup of tea just because I'm bored or can't decide what to do next. Pinning yourself down to a schedule helps to reduce the number of decisions you have to make, meaning less decision-making fatigue. Phew.

. . . .

Exercise: rehearsing your day

When you imagine things taking place, your brain is activated in exactly the same way as if those events are really happening, so it's a great way to prepare your mind for success. Before you begin the day, visualize and mentally rehearse in your mind how you'd like it to go. See yourself getting on with tasks with calm focus and confidence. Visualize things going well and the good feelings associated with that. Then imagine relaxing at the end of the day, feeling proud that you made good progress in your tasks.

. . . .

Decisions, decisions

• •

Exercise: **the Pomodoro technique**

This productivity and time-management technique was devised by Francesco Cirillo, who found that by breaking down tasks into manageable segments he was able to be way more productive. You can find out more about the method and ways to implement it at pomodorotechnique.com, but here are the basics:

- Get a timer (or use the timer on your phone) and set it for twenty-five minutes. You are going to focus solidly on one task – no distractions, no switching to something else, no checking social media. Some people find that having the timer ticking on their desk really focuses the mind. (Of course, if the ticking makes you anxious, use your phone timer instead!)
- When the alarm goes off, give yourself a five-minute break before moving on to the next twenty-five-minute block of work.
- It sounds simple, and it is, but this really works! Give it a try.

• •

Summary

★ Anxiety about making decisions often stems from fear of failure, but there's no such thing as the perfect decision. What matters is how you approach the outcome.

★ Too much choice can be a bad thing, and decision fatigue is very real. Consider stream-lining your life so that you have fewer decisions to make.

★ Intuitive decision-making is often just as effective as analytical reasoning, and way less exhausting than over-thinking everything. Trust your gut feelings.

★ Procrastination can be a way to protect our-selves from having to make a decision. It goes hand in hand with anxiety, but it can be tamed!

CHAPTER 6

Relax, nothing is under control

The quest for certainty blocks the search for meaning. Uncertainty is the very condition to impel man to unfold his powers.

ERICH FROMM, PSYCHOLOGIST

I'm embarrassed to admit this but at university my friends (lovingly) nicknamed me 'Sarge' (short for sergeant major), due to my controlling tendencies. Things had to be done in a certain way. If I didn't eat at set times or if I was late for something, I would freak out. I always had a huge feeling of tension inside of me and was (I now realize) desperately trying to control the uncontrollable, including the people around me. What's more, I felt I had to control *myself* around new people. I would suppress the real me in the hope that I could somehow control what they thought of me. The irony is that whenever I sensed myself getting worked up about all this, I actually felt *less* in control.

This excessive need for certainty can stem from a number of things, such as growing up with a controlling parent, suffering abuse or trauma, or feeling helpless or vulnerable. At its root is a fear of *losing* control. Being too busy and having too many plates spinning at once makes it worse. We feel unsafe because there are so many uncertain variables. In my case, when I had too much going on I would tighten my grip, micromanage and over-think every possible outcome as a way of feeling more secure and safe. It's no wonder I felt tense.

My client Andrea, thirty-seven, grew up with very con-trolling parents. They were so determined that she must do well at school that she wasn't allowed to go out and play with her friends; she always had to stay in and study. She tried to claw back some sense of being in control by being a very picky eater (not that she realized she was doing this at the time). When she reached adulthood she became a perfectionist, both with herself and others. This created a huge amount of anxiety, as she tried to meet her own impossible standards, and affected her relation-ships with other people who couldn't meet her expect-ations. She would have panic attacks over minor mishaps such as running late to work.

Another client, Simone, a twenty-six-year-old PR exec-utive in London, grew up with an alcoholic mother in a very chaotic environment, feeling uncertain and insecure. As an adult, she became a meticulous planner. Every detail of her day-to-day routine had to be thoroughly researched and mapped out in order for her to feel a sense of security. It was almost impossible for her to enjoy life because she just couldn't relax. If she didn't feel in control at all times, she would panic.

The problem is, there are so many things in life to be uncertain about: what career to aim for; how long your parents will be around; the state of the housing market; that restructuring going on at work. It's impossible to control *all* these things, if any of them! And anxiety itself makes you feel out of control – of your symptoms, your thoughts and feelings. What if you have a panic attack? Or desperately need to run to the loo because your nerves affect your tummy? Trying to control things outside of you keeps you in a vicious cycle of stress, all because you feel out of control inside your mind.

Go with the flow

You've probably been told before to 'let go and relax' or to 'go with the flow.' It might sound easy but it can feel like one of the hardest things to do. Our need to be in control, according to psychologists Joe Griffin and Ivan Tyrell, authors of *Human Givens: The New Approach to Emotional Health and Clear Thinking,* is linked to a fundamental and universal need to feel secure and safe. They explain that anxiety can be triggered by change, loss or new environments, leaving you feeling insecure. Your limbic brain believes it's keeping you safe by causing you to tense up, hold on tight, overthink everything and be on high alert. But as Joe and Ivan state in their book, 'We all live a transient life while pretending that life is constant.' We kid ourselves that it's possible to be in control, when really it isn't; we tell ourselves that control will give us certainty and security, which it can't.

But maybe things can be out of control and still be good. If everything was certain, there would be no excitement, no growth, no learning. Uncertainty boosts your confidence when you learn that you can, in fact, handle challenges. It forces you out of your comfort zone so you can expand to be your best self. When you push into the unknown, yes, you open yourself up to some level of risk – what if it doesn't work out? – but you also open yourself up to new possibilities and opportunities. The more accepting you become of uncertainty, the happier and calmer you can be.

I slowly learnt that being in control is overrated. Being controlling sabotages happiness and limits possibilities. These days, I reframe fear of uncertainty as excitement and try to see every situation as an opportunity for learning and growing. I find the following Serenity Prayer (which by now must have become the go-to mantra of all stressed-out millennials) very helpful:

Grant me the serenity to accept the things I cannot change,
Courage to change the things I can,
And wisdom to know the difference.

My client Lauren, thirty-two, a project manager from London, told me, 'I think anxiety and a need to be in control are very much linked. I have anxious thoughts because I try to control things that are impossible to control. Mindfulness and focusing on the exact moment I'm in helps me the most.' A fear of losing control is almost always about things in the future. When we come back to the present, we can cope with and respond to whatever is going on in that moment.

Expect the best but plan for the worst

Despite the fact that most of the things we worry about never happen, sometimes in life things *do* go wrong. We will all experience (temporary) failure, loss and challenges. So how can we prepare for these times in the most constructive way? In her book *The Positive Power of Negative Thinking: Using Defensive Pessimism to Harness Anxiety and Perform at Your Peak*, Julie Norem discusses a technique called 'defensive pessimism'. This involves mentally rehearsing the worst-case scenario in a calm and rational way, which helps you to feel more prepared if things do go wrong. The important part, though, is to imagine yourself handling it.

For example, say you have a presentation coming up. You imagine all the things that could go wrong: forgetting the words, the projector breaking, tripping up over the carpet. But as you imagine them, see yourself regaining your composure, doing the presentation without your slides and smoothly steadying yourself after your fall. In this way you remind yourself that, even if things go wrong, you can handle it. Because, sweetheart, you absolutely can.

Surrendering isn't giving up

Sometimes, being in control means deciding to let go. Things often happen more smoothly and easily when we allow them to unfold in their own time, rather than trying too hard to make them occur or to force them before they're ready.

Over the past few years I've been learning to loosen my grip. I used to feel I had to control things in order for them to *be good* and in order to feel happy. But the tense, tight, controlling sensation doesn't feel so good, so it sabotages the happiness it's trying to create.

There's a pose in yoga called 'pigeon pose', which was always horribly challenging for me. You sit on the floor with one leg stretched out behind you and your other shin out horizontally in front of you, while you (try) to lean forward. It stretches the psoas muscle in the hip and, if you're anything like me and used to sitting at a desk all day, this stretch can fall somewhere on the spectrum between damn hard work and absolute agony. During one class, after shuffling myself into the pose, I felt myself start to tense up and resist the discomfort of the stretch. I didn't want to feel it. I wished it would end. A mental battle was taking place between me and my body. I was pushing and straining my muscles, trying to force my hip to open up. The teacher must have recognized the grimace on my face because she came over and said gently, 'Just surrender into the pose.' At first, my inner critic thought, 'Nope, I'm not doing that,' but then, realizing I had no better option, I decided to give this surrendering thing a go. And I felt something release, first in my mind, then in my body. I let myself relax and surrendered to gravity as I flopped to the floor. I was letting my body be; I'd stopped trying to force it. It was such a relief! I felt like the battle had ended. As my body relaxed, so did my mental state and I immediately felt better.

These days, I try to practise surrender in other areas of life, too. Surrendering means letting go, allowing things to be as they are and trusting that everything will work out. If I'm nervous about making a presentation, then, once I get to the meeting, I remind myself to surrender to it, let go and remember that no matter what happens, I'll be OK. It's out of my control now. It's the mental and emotional equivalent of letting out a big sigh and allowing your shoulders to drop down. It feels so much better than forcing, controlling and being tense.

When we surrender to the symptoms of anxiety and just allow them to be there, without trying to change or control them, they will often start to change all by themselves. Surrendering to the circumstances of life means you can stop fighting against them and just let them be, trusting that things will work out.

Some of us find it hard to surrender because it can seem like giving up. But sometimes letting go means regaining control, and giving up the struggle is the most empowering thing we can do. If trying to control things all the time hasn't been working for you, isn't it time to try something different? When you surrender and flow with life, you relax, and when you relax you're more able to tune in to your intuition and creativity; it's easier to think clearly and solutions start to arise more easily.

. . . .

Exercise: surrender to what is

Think about a situation you need to surrender to. What would it be like if you could do this? How would it – and you – be different? How would that feel? Spend two minutes contemplating living your life without worrying about the outcome of any of your dilemmas or anxiety-making scenarios.

. . . .

Exercise: dig deep into control

Write down all the things you're trying to control. Now ask yourself these questions. Are there any particular areas or aspects of your life that you always try to control? Are there ways that controlling serves a pur-pose for you? And in what ways does it impact you negatively? How would a good friend 'answer back' to your worries? What advice or reassurance would they give you?

. . . .

Feel the fear

At the age of nine I went through the first of many transformations. There was a theme park near where we lived and its scariest ride was 'The Tower of Terror'. It involved going upside down in a loop-the-loop inside a haunted house. I was curious, but also afraid. It felt like a new frontier. After much 'umming and ahhing' I finally plucked up the courage to go on the ride. Yes, I clutched Dad's hand the whole time, but the thrill was incredible. I was such a cautious child, but now I had faced a fear and survived! After that I was much more confident; I knew I was capable of doing scary things and that I could cope with it. It was a small step, perhaps, but for me it had a huge impact. I stopped clutching the banister and leapt down the stairs two at a time, because I knew I could trust myself.

Many of us, from a young age, are told in blatant or subtler ways that the world is a treacherous place and we should be careful, fearful and risk-averse. Susan Jeffers' classic self-help book *Feel the Fear and Do it Anyway: How to Turn Your Fear and Indecision into Confidence and Action*, covers this. She says the implication is that we won't be able to handle the big, bad world. We learn not to trust ourselves. Susan says that everyone experiences fear (yup, even the most successful and confident-seeming people – hello Adele!), and the aim of the game is not to eliminate fear, which is impossible, but to get more comfortable with it while not allowing it to hold you back.

Anxiety is often linked to having a low tolerance for uncomfortable emotions. Which kind of makes sense. Who wants to feel tense and nervous as hell? Not me! We try to control our way out of having to feel those things. But getting comfortable with discomfort is a huge step if you want to overcome anxiety. The more you can stay with uncomfortable feelings, the more those feelings diminish.

When you are living a full and varied life, when you are setting challenges and growing as a person, you will inevitably experience some fear. Remember, just because we're frightened, that doesn't mean there is any real danger ahead. We need to feel the discomfort and move forward anyway. Doing this teaches the amygdala – the part of your brain responsible for the fight-or-flight response – that the perceived danger is not real. Learning that it's OK to feel afraid, that you will cope, is a fundamental step in freeing yourself of anxiety.

When you face your fears they usually diminish because you've either a) proven that you can in fact handle the feared situation and everything was fine, or b) if something did go a little wrong you've learnt that, even then, it's not actually as bad as you imagined. Again, you handled it – even as it went 'wrong'.

Always be kind to yourself when you're facing a fear or moving out of your comfort zone. You're massively brave for doing it and, no matter how it goes, you will get better, learn tons and grow as a person. Go you!

Expand your horizons

A client of mine recently told me she felt she was slowly expanding her circle of capability. Having suffered with fear and anxiety for years, her sphere of life had shrunk to the point where she only felt safe in bed. Once she had made the decision that she could no longer allow her fears to limit her so drastically, she very slowly began to push beyond her comfort zone and in the process learnt that she could handle things. She was able to gradually feel more confident and relaxed. She began to purposely put herself in new situations, get out and meet people and challenge herself in new ways. Although it was uncomfortable at first, every experience taught her something. Slowly, she learnt that she *was* capable and could trust herself. She discovered that she could adapt, think on her feet and handle things in the moment. What's more, she had to travel two hundred miles to come to her sessions with me, stay in a hotel and meet new people. In the past that would have scared her senseless. But she pushed past the fear, expanded her horizons and, now, who knows what she'll try next.

Susan Jeffers has a mantra that I particularly love. If there is an 'answer' to our uncertainties, this is it . . . '*No matter what happens, I'll handle it.*'

We all carry wisdom within us, made up of our experiences, everything we've learnt and our innate intelligence and instincts. There's something else, too. Our wisdom taps into the part of us that's been evolving for the past 4 billion years since life on Earth began, to make the incredible, capable and brilliant human being that is you. You will respond and adapt to whatever life throws your way and you can trust yourself to handle whatever crops up. If I ever find myself feeling afraid about an uncertain future, I come back to the idea that I might not know exactly *how* I'll handle whatever arises, but I trust that *I will be able to.*

Float, don't fight

The pioneering psychiatrist Carl Jung said, *'What you resist, persists.'* If you've ever attempted to force yourself to calm down when you're anxious, you'll know what he meant, because you probably wound up feeling even more tense. When you fight your feelings, they only end up getting stronger. No one's blaming you for trying to fight your anxiety, though. A racing heart, a torrent of worries and an impending sense of doom are uncomfortable at the best of times and friggin' terrifying at the worst. Our natural response is to try to make them stop. Like, now! Or even better, ten minutes ago! But the worst part is that we become afraid of the anxiety symptoms themselves. We make them mean all sorts of dire things. 'What's wrong with me? Am I going crazy? Am I going to die? I'll never be normal! It must mean I'm in real danger!' Everything we say and do ends up making us feel way worse. Our minds go into overdrive trying to problem-solve our way out of the sensations and we get stuck in a never-ending loop.

But here's another idea. Claire Weeks, doctor and author of *Self-Help for Your Nerves: Learn to Relax and Enjoy Life Again by Overcoming Stress and Fear*, invites us to 'float with the anxiety' rather than fighting it. Imagine you're in the sea and you're not so great at swimming. You struggle and thrash around, exhausting yourself, barely able to keep your head above water. If you were to let go, lay back and relax, you'd find that your body would naturally float without any effort or struggle. What would it be like to just allow the thoughts and sensations of anxiety to be there, without trying to control them or make them stop? To 'float' with anxiety rather than to fight it? By letting go and allowing the feelings to be there without needing to push them away, you stop the fight and the symptoms pass all by themselves. If what you resist persists, then what you allow dissolves.

The ultimate in losing control, for many people, would be to have a panic attack. We fear that we'll go crazy, have a heart attack or die. The symptoms make you feel seriously out of control; you may feel the need to run, your heart races, you might feel tingly, unable to breathe, dizzy or that you've become dissociated from your body. When I first had a panic attack I remember thinking that my body had gone totally berserk and I was just along for the ride. What I didn't understand was that all those symptoms are caused by adrenaline. And although an attack feels horrendous, it *isn't* actually dangerous. The mind has been tricked into thinking there is a threat, so it triggers a huge fight-or-flight response, even though there is no real danger. So if you find yourself experiencing a panic attack, try to reassure yourself that the symptoms are just caused by adrenaline and that the feeling *will* pass. Repeat the mantra, 'It's just adrenaline – I am safe.'

Lean in

Anxiety can make you want to avoid things, to 'lean back' from situations in an attempt to stay safe or avoid discomfort. But sometimes you need to take action to overcome your anxiety. By moving towards uncertainty you teach yourself a huge amount and grow in confidence in the process. Anxiety will tell you, 'I'm not ready,' 'I can't cope' or 'It's not safe'. But if you're waiting until you feel confident and safe before you take any action, you'll be waiting a long time. It's not true that you need to feel confident before you do something. Do it, and then the confidence will follow. In psychology, this is called 'exposure therapy', in other words, doing the things you're afraid to do. Worries shrink when you walk towards them.

A few years ago I went on holiday to the French Alps to learn to snowboard. Now, snowboarding was something I had resisted for a while. My boyfriend lives for snowboarding, I mean, totally obsessed, but I'd been massively put off by my experience a few years before when I first tried to ski. Anxiety had got the better of me. I was a tense, anxious mess. I hated the ski lifts, despised the steepness of the slopes and couldn't wait for the holiday to end. I'd mentally rehearsed my death a hundred times on that holiday: ending up in a frosty grave, mangled between the trees and my skis. I was sure I would never go back to the mountains after this experience. I was hyper-aware of the dangers and didn't trust my body. However, after a couple of years, some serious self-work and a dash of envy at seeing the holiday photos of all my friends enjoying the après-ski – in a hot tub, sipping Prosecco – I decided to give it another go. I knew it was only fear that was holding me back from joining in the fun and, with my new life-is-an-adventure mindset, I kitted myself out in knee and bum pads (the works!) and booked my flight.

This time I noticed several things that seemed to me like metaphors for life, especially for the anxious among us. If you ask anyone who has learnt to snowboard they will often tell you that the first week, or two or three, can be pretty demoralizing. You fall over. Again. And again. And again. It's physically exhausting, not to mention crushing for the spirit. Accepting that falling over is part of the process is all you can do. I started off on the baby slopes, which was pretty easy. There are no ski lifts to contend with, the slopes are gentle and your fellow snowboarders mostly comprise of super-cute four-year-olds in brightly coloured onesies. But by day three it was time to hit the big-girl slopes. These were steeper, the ski lifts were high and skiers whizzed by at thirty miles an hour as I stiffly battled to stay upright on my board.

The instructor kept telling me again and again to 'lean in'. The thing with snowboarding is that 'leaning in' down the hill is the only way to actually have control over the board. Doing this decreases the chance that you're going to fall over and makes it more likely you'll turn successfully. But fear makes you instinctively want to lean back.

'Chloe, you're too scared, you keep leaning back, you're too tense!' the instructor yelled at me repeatedly. I was well aware of how on edge I was. When you're facing down a hill of hard, slippery ice, leaning in feels like a totally counterintuitive thing to do. Why would I want to lean towards a slick, treacherous hill?! My adrenaline surged and I felt an overwhelming desire to run away to a warm, safe place. My amygdala had switched on the fight-or-flight response. My heart raced, I felt sick and my knees were wobbly.

One thing I've learnt about women who have anxiety is that we have a problem leaning in to things in general, whether it's speaking up, taking risks or putting ourselves out there. Leaning in can feel risky and unsafe. It means stepping into the unknown; we don't trust ourselves and, yup, we're afraid of losing control. But leaning into life, taking on challenges, pushing ourselves a little out of our comfort zones and taking a few risks is essential if we're to overcome anxiety. It teaches us that we *can* cope. When you do something you're scared to do, and you handle it, it gives you the sort of confidence boost that nothing else can. As a result, you feel in control – ironic, as you probably felt out of control doing the thing that scared you! – and you bolster your self-belief.

At the beginning of that holiday, every time I pushed off on my snowboard I pulled back at the last moment, terrified of the steep slope ahead. But I stayed with the feeling. I stayed on the slope, even though I felt scared. When we stay with an anxious feeling rather than running away or avoiding the situation, we teach ourselves that the situation is not in fact as dangerous as we think it is. Eventually, the fight-or-flight response starts to reduce and the amygdala becomes less reactive. We teach our brains that the situation isn't a life-or-death one and learn that we are capable, that we can trust ourselves.

As the days went on my confidence grew. I knew that if I fell over I could just get back up again. It wasn't as bad as my anxious brain had made it out to be. I learnt something from every fall and got better and better every day. By the end of the holiday I felt unstoppable. It gave me a huge confidence boost; if I'd overcome this fear, what else was I capable of? I felt ready to go out of my comfort zone in other areas of my life. When it comes to overcoming fears and stepping into the unknown, we need to 'feel the fear and do it anyway', as Susan Jeffers says.

Self-help author Byron Katie tells a story about being in the desert and coming across what she was convinced at first sight was a snake. It took her a while to realize that, actually, it was a rope, because her terror was literally making her see things that weren't there. When we're anxious we see snakes everywhere. The anxiety makes us think that things are dangerous, but 99.9 per cent of the time there's no danger at all. So next time your anxious mind tries to tell you something is dangerous or that you should be fearful, say to yourself, *'It's only a rope.'*

I can't stress enough how important it is *not* to avoid the situations and things that make you anxious. Doing so only makes anxiety worse. If you spend your life avoiding things, not only will you miss out on loads of great opportunities and experiences, but if there comes a day when you do have to face your fear, it will be one hundred times worse. Whether it's being in large crowds, flying in an aeroplane, going to a party where you don't know many people or speaking in public, when you lean in, the fear slowly recedes. It might not be comfortable, but it's necessary for you to move forward.

· ·

Exercise: leaning in to life

What do you need to 'lean in' to in your life? Could you say yes to something you've previously been reluctant or fearful to do? Could you put yourself out there in some way? Make a request for something that you want? Finally make that decision? Do something you've been putting off? *Feel the fear and take action anyway.* Make some notes on what small actions you could take to start leaning in to your fear and anxiety. It doesn't need to be anything huge. Just think about what the first step would be and then the next. Take baby steps at first and your confidence *will* grow.

· ·

Summary

★ The answer to most of your uncertainties is: *'No matter what happens, I'll handle it.'*

★ Float with anxiety rather than trying to fight it.

★ Sometimes, surrendering and letting go is the best way to regain a sense of control.

★ Don't avoid the things that scare you. Taking action and leaning in to situations increases your confidence because you learn that you *can* cope. It teaches your brain that the situation is not actually dangerous and so it reduces the fight-or-flight response.

CHAPTER 7

It's all about the brain – not the ass!

To those struggling with anxiety, OCD,
depression: I know it's madly annoying when
people tell you to exercise, and it took me
about sixteen medicated years to listen,
but I'm glad I did. It ain't about the ass,
it's about the brain.

LENA DUNHAM, ON INSTAGRAM

Whether you're a complete workout noob or already working out like a fiend, this chapter will give you more motivation and inspiration to start (or carry on) getting a sweat on, not just for the fab body benefits but for the amazing mind-relaxing results.

NHS experts have said that if exercise came in pill form, it would be one of the most cost-effective drugs ever produced. The benefits of exercise are many, from improved self-esteem and a sense of overall wellbeing to lower risk of disease, depression and stress.

But if the thought of intense training seems decidedly unrelaxing, there's good news. NHS guidelines state that light, moderate and high-intensity exercise can *all* reduce your level of anxiety. Light exercise would be something like gentle walking, moderate means you could hold a conversation but definitely not sing during the activity, while high intensity is when there's no way you can chat because you're working so damn hard! The NHS recommends we all take thirty minutes of moderate exercise five days a week. That could be brisk walking, bike riding, swimming or tennis.

Sounds easy in theory, right? But if three flights of stairs feels like your own personal Everest, remember to go easy on yourself and start slowly. Even Jessica Ennis-Hill had to start somewhere. Whatever you do, please don't allow fitness – or lack thereof – to be another reason to beat yourself up. Don't add it to your list of shoulds – 'I should have gone for a run but I didn't so that means I'm bad/lazy/unmotivated/useless.' It ought to be fun – playful, even – and something you do for yourself with love, not as a form of punishment.

I spoke to personal trainer Matt Roberts, who counts Amanda Holden, the Saturdays and Mel C among his clients. 'The evidence in support of regular exercise for a healthy body and mind is overwhelming,' he told me. 'There's a lot of confusion created by the fitness industry about what the best approach is and this can often lead to people obsessing about the details and losing focus on the bigger picture. If you find a way that helps you to remain consistently active, regardless of your choice of exercise, that's what counts and leads to the biggest pay-off. It's about setting yourself up in a way that means you guarantee success.'

Consistency is key, in other words. So is enjoying it, as it means you're more likely to stick at it. And if you are unfit right now, the good news is you could have the most to gain from exercise. In fact, it's been shown that the less physically fit and the more anxious you are, the greater the benefit you can expect.[1]

The science part

Studies have demonstrated that exercising lowers the activity of the sympathetic nervous system[2] – the fight-or-flight response – which explains why after you've been to the gym you typically feel more relaxed, safe and at ease. We all need this! And there's more positive brain chemistry at work. That fantastic high after an adrenaline-pumped spin class or a glowsticks-wielding clubbercise class is all down to endorphins. When you exert yourself through high-intensity exercise your body produces chemicals that are similar in their structure to opiates (such as morphine) and can create a euphoric feeling, or at least a boost in your mood. It's thought they are re-leased to help you manage any pain, such as sore feet and aching muscles, and are responsible for that much-sought-after 'runner's high'. Endorphins are part of the reason exercise is so good for calming anxiety, because after-wards you are inevitably in a better mood.

Another example of the mood-boosting and eventual calming benefits of exercise, this time in cold water, was discovered in the early twentieth-century. Psychiatric patients were often given cold baths, or 'hydrotherapy', to calm them down. It was thought the cold water reduced blood flow to their brains, reducing mental over-activity. Additionally, the 'shock' of being exposed to the cold water was believed to jolt them out of their agitated mental state. If this sounds outdated, Professor Mike Tipton from the University of Portsmouth has theorized that exposure to cold water really can improve the way we respond to stress. The idea was explored in an episode of the BBC documentary series *Trust Me, I'm a Doctor* in September 2016, when Dr Chris van Tulleken helped a patient with depression boost her mood by doing laps of a lake. But if cold-water swimming isn't an option for you, just switching the shower to cold for a minute or two could help you to glean some of the benefits. Lots of self-help motivational speakers, including Tony Robbins and Tim Ferriss, practise this cold-water 'therapy' to boost their immune systems and moods. Tony has spoken about the cold-water plunge pool at his house, which he uses daily.

Numerous studies point to the fact that exercise causes changes in brain chemistry and brain structure to make you calmer. One study at Princeton University, carried out on mice, compared sedentary rodents with ones that were allowed to run on a wheel. The 'runner' mice were found to have higher levels of the neurotransmitter GABA, which has been shown to calm the brain. (Think of GABA as something that tells your over-anxious brain cells to chill out – who doesn't want that?). They were more able to handle stress and showed signs of greater confidence and reduced anxiety.[3]

Animal studies have also shown that exercise helps the brain repair itself from the effects of stress. It causes shiny new cells to be made in a part of the brain called the hippocampus – the part that can become damaged as a result of repeated exposure to the stress hormones adrenaline and cortisol, as would be the case with chronic stress.[4] Basically, exercise has a very real and positive effect on your nervous system, on the structure of your brain and its neurochemistry. It's win, win, win!

Zap your exercise worries

It's all very well to be convinced of the benefits in theory. But let's face it, lots of people know they should exercise and still find excuses to put it off. And if you've ever experienced a panic attack, the memory might be warning you off digging out your running shoes. After all, exertion can create a similar heart-pounding sensation, and it's easy to associate that feeling with danger. 'Anxiety sensitivity' is when you believe that the symptoms of anxiety, including a rapid heartbeat, are in themselves harmful – even though, in fact, they aren't. If you are resisting exercise because of fear, take comfort from a 2008 study which found that doing aerobic exercise actually made participants *more* comfortable and *less* afraid of the symptoms of anxiety.[5] By getting your heart pumping you can teach yourself to be OK with that sensation. You learn that although it's not very pleasant to feel your heart thumping in your chest like an 808 drum turned up to eleven, it's not actually going to do you any harm.

If you're still struggling with the motivation to exercise, try thinking about it as something fun and playful rather than another chore to cross off your to-do list. I spoke to Nicola, thirty-one, a yoga teacher and social media manager, who said, 'When I'm feeling anxious I exercise with the intention of connecting to my inner child – a state that's happy, light-hearted and calm. I make sure I choose an activity I enjoy and that's fun, not just one I think is good for training purposes. I focus on the breath and how it feels rather than how it looks or what the "numbers" are, i.e. how many calories I'm burning. This helps me focus on being in my body and being present again, which combats the anxiety. For me, walking, yoga, cycling and running are proving effective.'

For some of us, exercise feels like yet another thing we have to be good at, another area of life where we will feel awkward and out of place. Perfectionists and people who suffer social anxiety are likely to dread the gym, or the dance class or the running club. Perhaps you're worried you won't know how to use the machines or that you don't have the 'right' gear or you're embarrassed about becoming a sweaty, hot mess.

'Gym-timidation' is real but, rest assured, the vast majority of gym-goers are focused on one thing and one thing only – themselves. If you have to spend a few minutes trying to fathom how to use the cross trainer, or you wobble as you get into a lunge, no one is going to notice or care. Allow yourself to be a beginner; you don't have to be amazing at this straight away. You have to start somewhere, so go easy on yourself. Wear your hot-messiness like a badge of honour. You rock that look! It's a sign that you're growing stronger and fitter, both physically and mentally. The trick is to feel the discomfort and to stay with it.

I remember the first time I walked into the weights room at my gym. I was so self-conscious and nervous. The place was filled with huge, muscly men wearing string vests (I'm not even kidding). Everyone seemed to know what they were doing. I wanted to run away and curl up in a dark room! Then I reminded myself why I was there: to do something amazing and positive for myself. So I stayed put, even though I felt nervous. These days, I breeze into the gym without a care in the world; I'm so focused on my workout that I barely even notice the vest-wearers any more. You can do that, too!

Natasha, a twenty-nine-year-old librarian, told me, 'I have a fair amount of social anxiety. When I started British Military Fitness I would worry about being good enough, what other people thought of me and whether I'd be able to do all the exercises, or even keep up. But I loved the fact it was outdoors, and being with other people made it fun. Being so active took my mind off my anxiety and I soon relaxed into it and made friends.'

The social aspect that Natasha identified is important. Like most things in life, exercise is way better with a friend by your side. If going to the gym or to a class is scary at first, having a wingman or woman there with you can give you the confidence to try something new. Plus, you can't let your exercise buddy down so you'll be more likely to continue – or even show up in the first place! Exercising with a friend or joining a group class multiplies the mental-health-boosting benefits, too. Anxiety can feel so isolating at times; it can make you want to hide away and stay at home. But given that more than 20 per cent of women feel anxious most of the time, according to the Mental Health Foundation's 2014 report, chances are that at any exercise class or group others will be feeling the same as you. Exercising in a group or with someone else gives you an external focus and something to talk about as you build up your social confidence. The science even backs this up; a study at Oxford University found that exercising with others increases levels of mood-boosting endorphins more than exercising alone.[6]

Get in the zone and out of your head

Anxiety can feel like being trapped in your head and sometimes you'll do anything to get out of it. Maybe, like me, you've turned to booze or food. Maybe you've used drugs to quieten those voices and numb your pain. Exercise is one of the best, and healthiest, ways of getting out of your head. Natasha told me, 'A lot of my worries – things such as "I'm not good enough," "I don't earn enough," and "how will I afford a mortgage?" – stop mattering so much when I work out because I'm too busy trying to complete each exercise.' Working out quietens your anxious brain because it forces you to be present and focus on what your body is doing in the moment. It's much easier to forget about worries when you're trying to keep up with the Zumba moves!

Athletes often talk about getting 'in the zone' – a state of flow where you feel fantastic, fully immersed in the moment and less conscious of yourself and your thoughts (which, when you're anxious, can only be a good thing). Mihaly Csikszentmihalyi, author of *Flow: The Psychology of Happiness*, believes people are at their happiest when in 'a state of concentration or complete absorption with the activity at hand and the situation'. Exercise is a great way to get there, as are other activities such as writing, playing music and dancing. Sounds pretty good, right?

Health editor Katy Sunnassee, thirty-seven, told me that during her early twenties, when she experienced a period of severe anxiety and stress, salsa dancing or jogging along the beach were the only ways of lifting the grip anxiety had on her. She spent months locked into a cycle of repetitive negative thinking, worrying about both major and minor decisions. It was salsa dancing that was her saviour. 'Even now, it totally takes me out of my head and into my body. I can't help but smile when I dance, as I so love the music and moving my body to the rhythm.

What's more, you *have* to be in the moment, or in the flow, to connect with your partner and follow his lead. It's the ultimate stress buster and mood booster.'

Build your self-belief

You know that feeling of achievement and self-assurance you get when you cope with a challenge or do something well? Psychologist Albert Bandura gave it a name: self-efficacy. It's that glow you get when you complete a tough Pilates class, perfect your tennis serve or master a tricky dance move. It's a boost of self-belief and confidence that says, 'I've got this.' The more self-efficacy we have, the less anxious we're likely to feel.[7]

Health editor Katy told me how this feeling of accomplishment gave her a massive boost when she really needed it. 'I was rehearsing for a salsa performance, and there was a bit in the routine that entailed us girls doing handstands in front of our partners. They were supposed to catch our ankles and then we had to flip up on to their shoulders. I was totally freaked out when I saw the teachers do it. I thought, "There is no way on earth I'll ever be able to do that." My first attempts were horrendous. I couldn't even kick my legs up high enough and just did a load of pony kicks! I was so scared of falling on my face and hurting myself. But one day, when no one was looking – other than my partner – I told myself, 'Oh just f**king do it!', and you know what? I did! I kicked my legs all the way up into a handstand and managed to flip myself up – that was actually the easy part, as I have strong stomach muscles. The hard bit was trusting myself, and my arms! Anyway, the feeling of euphoria was incredible. I felt invincible! I could barely even do a forward roll as a child so that handstand was the most gymnastic thing my body had ever done. Doing it again and again in front of crowds at salsa clubs across London as we performed our routine was amazing. Even though now, four years later, I've lost the ability to do a handstand – if you don't use it, you lose it, after all – I'll never forget the excitement I felt doing it for the first time.'

Exercise is a really effective way to increase self-efficacy and self-esteem and you don't need to do handstands to get your own personal boost. Whether you try a new class, reach 10,000 daily steps or finally get yourself up to running a 5K, it's the small wins that help you prove to yourself you *are* capable. It's been shown that exercising at a moderate intensity actually gives you the most benefits because you get a sense of achievement without it being so hard you risk failure.[8] So don't try to go from zero to a marathon in one week; build up slowly and watch your confidence grow. Setting yourself small, achievable exercise challenges could pay off big time in how confident and capable you feel in your life in general. And it'll kick stress and anxiety to the kerb with every step you take.

Shake off the stress

According to trauma expert Peter Levine in his book *Waking the Tiger: Healing Trauma – The Innate Capacity to Transform Overwhelming Experiences,* animals in the wild shake themselves violently after experiencing an episode of stress or fear. He uses the example of a gazelle, when it has survived being chased by a lion. It literally 'shakes off' the shock and tension to discharge the excess energy and adrenaline that the fight-or-flight response created. As for humans, we tend to hold on to that shit! We create tension in our bellies, shoulders, hips and necks from stress, panic or fear, and then carry it around with us.

Exercise is a great way of getting rid of that tension as it 'burns off' the excess adrenaline that is produced when you're anxious and removes the stress hormones that have accumulated in your blood which leave you feeling tense and restless. So exercise is known to be a great relaxant, but how about adding some shaking into your routine? I'm not necessarily suggesting you do this at your desk after a tense quarterly review with your boss, but when you can, whenever you experience a shock, angry outburst from someone or a tense train journey, try shaking it off by shaking your whole body, even if it's just for a few seconds. An accompanying soundtrack of Taylor Swift's 'Shake it Off' or Outkast's 'Hey Ya' is optional (but recommended!). It's an almost instant way to feel calmer and less tense.

There is a whole area of therapy called Trauma Release Therapy (TRE) that involves getting the body to shake as a means of casting off trauma; check out the videos on YouTube if you're keen to learn more, or Google local classes or practitioners.

Get back to nature

Could you be suffering from 'nature deficit disorder'? (Yes, it's a thing.) We all know that our bodies were not designed to sit still indoors all day in front of a computer screen. We need daylight, trees and fresh air to feel our best. A 2013 study done at the University of Essex and published by the mental health charity MIND[9] found that nearly 70 per cent of us experience 'significant increases in wellbeing' following 'eco-therapy' (that's getting out and doing things in nature, to you and me). The University of Exeter Medical School also looked at 1,000 people living in urban areas and discovered that those who moved to a place with green spaces had better mental health, including lower levels of anxiety and depression, than those who lived in less green areas. The conclusion? Being outside, even if it's only in a city park rather than the wilderness, is seriously good for your mental state. Exercising in the great outdoors gives you a double whammy of calm-inducing benefits. Try a jog in the park, a walk in the countryside, a park-based exercise class, a cycle ride through meadows, or even a swim in the sea, if you're brave (and live close to the coast). There's nothing like being surrounded by a big, open sky, huge trees and incredible wildlife for helping you to get things into perspective. Being immersed in nature helps you feel connected to something bigger than yourself, and your everyday problems or worries can seem less significant.

Find the thing you love to do

Personal trainer Matt Roberts told me that finding an activity that you enjoy is key to building exercise into your life. If you hate the gym, go swimming. If group sports remind you of anxious schooldays, take up running. If yoga makes you feel intimidated . . . Actually, if the thought of doing downward dogs is more anxiety-inducing than reducing, please bear with me. I'm convinced yoga is for everyone and I hope to convince you, too. The point is, there's something out there for all of us, so keep looking until you find it. Here are a few ideas to get you started.

The wonders of walking

Walking is such a simple everyday thing that it's hard to imagine it could have any impact when you're feeling seriously anxious. But actually, it's one of the best things you can do. Going for a stroll can take you away from whatever is triggering your anxiety. It provides a distraction so that, instead of stewing in worries, you're up, about, moving and doing something positive for yourself. If you've been tense, walking relaxes your muscles and helps you to loosen up.

According to the NHS, doing 10,000 steps a day makes you officially an 'active' person. Tracking the number of steps you take in a day has the effect of 'gamifying' walking and is really motivating. Many of us have pedometers built into our phones, so why not use yours and challenge yourself to reach a steps goal? Fitbits and other wearable tech are also great options for making any activity more fun. Matt advises that, as with all exercise, 'The key is to start small and build from there. Try a walk around the block. Make your walking goal small enough to simply get started and see whether you can go a bit further each time.'

Run (like the wind!)

Aerobic exercise such as running can help you use up any excessive adrenaline from stressing. It can also trigger a dose of those aforementioned endorphins. But in order to get the endorphin hit it's necessary to push yourself a bit – just enough so that your body produces the pain-relieving chemicals but not so much that you're stressing yourself out!

I spoke to Leah, a personal stylist aged thirty-four, who told me, 'I took up running to change my lifestyle and manage anxiety. It's helped me to eat better and drink less alcohol and means I now take better care of myself because I have to be fit to run. I ended up joining a running club and have now run a couple of marathons! Running helps me cope and takes my mind off things. I just feel better when I run. An unexpected benefit was meeting so many people and making new friends from all walks of life who have similar problems and symptoms. Being able to share things with people who can relate to my situation has really helped.'

Say yes to yoga

From the outside, yoga can seem pretty intimidating. *Yogis of Instagram* make it look so easy, gracefully swooping from pose to pose, whereas we imagine ourselves looking like drunken Twister players. But trust me when I say, everyone starts somewhere. I often hear people say, 'I can't do yoga; I'm too inflexible,' or 'I can't touch my toes, it's not for me!' You do *not* need to be slim, flexible or kitted out in the latest Lululemon garb to do yoga!

I'll always remember the sense of relief I felt when a teacher told me, 'Yoga is a breathing exercise. That's it.' When I remind myself of this I remember why I'm doing it. It's not to get slimmer thighs but to bring my mind into balance. Any booty-toning side effects are a fringe benefit. Remember that you're doing it for you, not to compete with anyone else. I like to position myself at the front of the class so I'm free from any distractions about what other people are doing and can focus purely on my own practice. And if you're sceptical or anxious about trying yoga, it really is worth getting past those feelings because, though there hasn't yet been enough research to conclusively prove that yoga combats anxiety, there is promising evidence that it does.[10]

My client Natasha uses yoga to manage her anxiety. 'Yoga helps me figure out what's bothering me. I don't do it to become *good* at it – I will not be doing headstands or anything like that! It's just a quiet space where I can focus on myself.'

Acclaimed yoga teacher Nadia Narain, who counts Kate Moss and Jules Oliver among her clients, told me, 'Yoga helps lessen anxiety by bringing you into your body and connecting you to your breath. One of the major things with anxiety is that you are disconnected from yourself and feel out of control. But with yoga, you learn to connect to yourself. Your breath brings you into the present moment, instead of your mind reeling.'

There are so many styles of yoga that you're bound to find one that suits your vibe. From hot to hatha, Ashtanga to restorative, yin to vinyasa, there's something for everyone. But don't let this abundance paralyse you – just find a local class that's easy for you to get to, and go. The most important thing, as with every form of exercise, is to start small and treat it as something fun. If you don't get on with one class, try another.

Time to team up

Playing a sport with others can be a great exercise option, particularly if you need help to overcome social anxiety.

The focus on the activity helps to distract your attention away from yourself and your worries, and it's a great way to interact with people and build your social confidence. My client Stephanie plays basketball and finds it really alleviates her anxiety. 'I admit I had to force myself to go at first – it was painful! But as I keep pushing myself out of my comfort zone I become more comfortable each week. I have to remember to be kind to myself in those moments when I do feel awkward and to feel proud of myself that I'm doing something scary but really positive for myself.'

. . . .

Exercise: making time to move

Brainstorm some ideas of types of exercise you'd like to try. Maybe something you used to love as a child? Or something new that's been intriguing you? Can you enlist a friend to exercise with you? Then set yourself a small goal: it might be to have a trial session at the gym with the aim of building up to run 10k, or booking a beginners' yoga class. Schedule something into your diary now and make it official. Also think about how you can walk more. Can you incorporate some walking into your journey to or from work? Could you have a walk at lunchtime? What about at weekends? Again, schedule it in your diary.

. . . .

Summary

★ Exercise is one of the best things you can do to manage anxiety; it lowers stress hormones, helps your brain to recover from over-worrying, produces mood-boosting endorphins and quietens mental chatter.

★ Treat exercise as an aspect of self-care, not as another thing on your to-do list. Find something you love to do.

★ Start slowly and build up. Remember, everyone has to start somewhere.

★ For best results, exercise outdoors and/or with a friend.

CHAPTER 8

Eating to beat anxiety

> One cannot think well, love well, sleep well,
> if one has not dined well.
>
> **VIRGINIA WOOLF**

If you're thinking, 'Wait, I already have enough worries about food without having to add in a crazy-strict, anti-anxiety food plan,' don't worry – this chapter is on your side! It's not about banning food groups or imposing rules. One of the most damaging ways we relate to food is our tendency to set up eating as being either virtuous or sinful. Since when was dinner a moral question, or a task we could either win or lose at? But what you put into your body *does* have an impact on your brain and moods. The chemical make-up of each thing you eat has the potential to impact your brain chemistry, hormones and mental state. So it's worth paying attention to what you eat and how it makes you feel and then making tweaks where you can to optimize the good feelings and minimize the bad ones.

A lot of the time we focus (read, obsess) on what we

shouldn't be eating but we also get seduced by the idea that if we only add in a couple of 'superfoods', all our health worries and anxieties will be cured. It's lovely to think that you can pop a food supplement or cut out one particular food item and . . . poof! . . . all your anxiety woes will be over. Of course, supplementation can make a difference, but it has to be a part of a bigger plan. The solution for anxiety is to do a few small things that add up to a big, positive change.

Rather than launch straight into telling you what to cut out and what to eat more of, I want to start from first principles about making food a positive, pleasurable, anxiety-relieving part of your life. As with exercise, try to see your diet as an aspect of self-love and self-care. Keep it in proportion. What you eat is important, sure, but it's really no big deal if you have a massive bowl of pasta or ice cream (or even both in one meal) once in a while. There's no need to beat yourself up. Don't let your diet be another source of anxiety, just do your best with it. And remember to enjoy your food!

As Amelia Freer, nutritional therapist and author of *Eat. Nourish. Glow*, told me, 'Set aside some time to invest in cooking and caring for yourself. You deserve it. It is the best form of self-care I know. And you will be blown away by the difference it makes.'

Eat like you love yourself

Can eating be a way of boosting self-esteem? Whenever you 'eat like you love yourself' you're sending a message to yourself about how much you value *you*. Think about it: how does eating a bag of chips on the hoof compare with sitting down to a carefully prepared healthy, fresh meal? And if you're doing the former, what does that say about how much you value yourself and your experience of eating? Shovelling down donuts as we zone out in front of the telly might seem like relaxing after a stressful day while we're doing it, but afterwards it can feel like we've abused our poor bodies rather than nurtured them. Eating well sends your subconscious a powerful message that 'I am worthy' and this sense of worthiness and enough-ness is essential when you're tackling anxiety.

Even if you're not yet at the point of loving yourself (it's a journey!), act *as if* you already do. Ask yourself, 'How would I eat if I really loved myself?' For me, eating like I love myself usually means making time for myself, setting the table and preparing something from fresh ingredients that are alive and bursting with colour, then giving myself the time to really taste and enjoy the food. It also means having the odd treat – I make no secret of my love for dark chocolate – but if I'm eating like I love myself, I take the time to really savour each bite and I don't beat myself up about it afterwards!

Mindful eating

Ah, mealtimes. An opportunity for quiet reflection, savouring your food and a break from work and worry . . . What?! Let's face it, often we eat with one eye on the phone and the other on the computer, a child or the TV, and we're more likely to inhale our food than relish it.

If you're feeling anxious, trying to multitask when you eat will only make matters worse. It's time to reclaim mealtimes! The simple act of stepping away from your laptop at lunch and putting down your phone during breakfast could have a huge effect on your state of mind, as well as helping you digest your food more easily.

In his book *Savor: Mindful Eating, Mindful Life*, Buddhist monk and mindfulness master Thich Nhat Hanh reminds us that 'anxiety comes primarily from our inability to dwell in the present moment.' What if savouring our food could help us to be less anxious? What if mealtimes were a chance to get present, reconnect with our bodies and have a well-earned mental break? I know for a fact that if I'm multitasking and eating, I feel more tense. Surfing news sites or catching up on *Game of Thrones* is enough to make anyone into a ball of anxiety. Mealtimes are an opportunity to slow down, get present and allow your digestive system to do its job. I promise you'll feel calmer and enjoy your food more if you do this. You can't lose.

So this is my invitation to you: have a distraction-free meal. Focus all your attention on enjoying your food. Set the table properly. Notice the appearance of your food on the plate – the colours and textures. Give it a good sniff to take in the aromas. Slowly take a bite and savour each taste and texture. Put down your knife and fork every so often and just . . . chew. Chew some more. Then chew a few more times. Reconnect with how full you feel. Feels better, right? *Ommm*.

Healthy gut, healthy mind

Your gut is an interesting place, to say the least. We've all experienced 'gut feelings', but did you know the gut is often called the second brain? With good reason. It houses 100 million brain cells, all within a surface area the size of a tennis court. (You read that right – there's brain tissue in your gut. It's no wonder things can go wrong in there.) What goes on in your belly can have a serious impact on how you think and feel. The majority of your serotonin – the happy and calm hormone – is made in the gut, and a 2013 study found that gut bacteria also has an effect on the production of GABA, the neurotransmitter that calms the brain.[1] A healthy gut is a healthy mind!

A lot of gut health comes down to the balance of 'good' and 'bad' bacteria. The gut is home to more than 100 trillion bacteria[2] (which is more than there are cells in your body, by the way!), and though some of those bugs can cause infection, many more of them are essential for digestion. Studies suggest that having plenty of the good bacteria can have an impact on your mental health. Researchers found that giving rats a supplement of a *bifidobacteria* probiotic meant they produced fewer stress hormones,[3] while a 2015 study done on humans found that another strain of *bifidobacteria* reduced levels of anxiety and even improved memory.[4] Research has also found that stress in early life can alter our gut bacteria and might be a contributing factor in anxiety later down the road.[5]

Sounds alarming, but there is good news. There are things we can do to influence the mix of our gut bacteria. So how do we boost good bacteria and give ourselves the best chance of good mental health? I suggest including both prebiotic and probiotic foods, as well as considering a probiotic supplement. And to reduce the bad stuff, try to limit your sugar intake – sugar feeds the 'bad' bacteria.

Prebiotics

Consuming prebiotic foods has been shown to lower levels of cortisol, a key stress hormone.[6] They also feed the good bugs in our bellies. Great sources are garlic, onion, leeks and chives (ideally raw, eek!), as well as peas, avocado, asparagus and Jerusalem artichokes.

Probiotics

Eating probiotic foods is a great way to introduce more good bacteria into your digestive system. Food sources that contain live bacteria include natural yoghurt, kefir (a fermented milk drink), sauerkraut (fermented cabbage, which is an acquired taste but great once you get used to it!) and kimchi (a Korean fermented-vegetable mix). Probiotic supplements such as those containing *lactobacillus* and *bifidobacterium* also offer a good mix of strains.

Eat to reduce inflammation

Inflammation of all kinds of body tissue is bad news for numerous aspects of our health. It's been linked to an increased risk of cancer[7] and heart disease.[8] And there is more and more evidence to suggest that chronic inflammation in the nervous system can increase our risk of anxiety.[9]

Dr Kelly Brogan shows in her book *A Mind of Your Own: The Truth About Depression and How Women Can Heal Their Bodies to Reclaim Their Lives* that inflammation can be caused by stress, eating sugar, fried foods and hydrogenated fats, chemicals in our diets and environment, or an imbalance of good and bad bacteria in the gut. Our immune systems' response creates the inflammation that in the long term can end up damaging our nervous systems and stopping them from functioning optimally. If a joint such as your elbow is inflamed, it can't work properly. It's like that for your brain, too. If the neurones in your brain are chronically inflamed, they just don't work as well.

Your anti-inflammatory diet

The following foods help to reduce inflammation in your entire body, which is not only great for general health but could help you reduce inflammation in your brain and nervous system and therefore potentially help with anxiety symptoms. As well as tweaking your diet, you might want to consider taking an omega-3 supplement. A 2011 study on medical students found that there was a 20 per cent decrease in anxiety levels after taking a fish-oil supplement, compared with a placebo.[10]

Include lots of these foods

- Green, leafy vegetables, such as spinach and kale
- Broccoli
- Berries, such as blueberries
- Nuts, such as almonds or walnuts
- Omega-3-containing foods, such as oily fish or flax seeds
- Coconut oil
- Turmeric (a bright yellow Indian spice)
- Ginger

Try to limit these foods

- Fried foods, such as chips, crisps and onion rings
- Foods containing hydrogenated fats, such as shop-bought biscuits, cakes and pastries
- Refined sugar

- Refined grains, such as white bread and pasta
- Processed meat, i.e. salami, ham and bacon

Anxiety and irritable bowel syndrome

Before I go on to talk about particular foods and their possible links to anxiety, I have to make a pause to talk about this widespread condition that straddles the gut / mind connection. Irritable bowel syndrome, or IBS, is characterized by recurring diarrhoea, constipation, bloating or stomach cramps. Despite the fact that it affects 23 per cent of UK women,[11] it's often not talked about and the embarrassment can add to the distress of the problem. Like anxiety, it's twice as likely to affect women as it is men.

Stress and anxiety seem to be linked to IBS (remember all those neurons in the gut?). They're not only a cause of IBS; the IBS can, in turn, create a lot of anxiety, so it's a vicious circle. If you're fearful about getting caught short on a shopping trip or you have to run out of a meeting to go to the loo urgently, or you're so bloated your stomach looks like a balloon, it's going to make you feel pretty miserable. IBS is inconvenient at best and devastating at worst and can have a huge impact on day-to-day life.

Managing anxiety by applying the techniques in this book could well have a positive impact on your IBS, but there are a few diet things that will probably help, too.

Everyone's digestive system works a little differently so it's important to keep a food and symptom diary (you can download one in the online bonuses section) to track how any changes you make might affect your symptoms. And as a note, if you suspect you have IBS, always speak to your doctor to rule out any other potential health issues. Here are a few pointers to get you thinking about possible links between your diet and your symptoms.

- For some people, high-fat or spicy foods can be a trigger; for others, wheat or dairy can be the problem. Experiment with cutting just one thing out for a whole week and track how it affects your symptoms.
- If you suffer with constipation, increasing the amount of soluble fibre you eat may help. Foods containing soluble fibre include oats, fruits such as apples and bananas, and golden linseeds. Make sure you drink plenty of water, as soluble fibre absorbs water and bulks things out and this is what gives it its laxative effect. And if that doesn't work, dose up on prunes!
- If diarrhoea is your trouble it may help to reduce the amount of insoluble fibre you eat. Insoluble fibre can increase the frequency of going to the loo by stimulating and irritating the bowel. Cut back on wholegrains, high-fibre breakfast cereals and nuts and seeds (except

golden linseeds) along with the skin, pips and pith of fruits and veggies – and definitely steer clear of those prunes!

- Eat slowly and chew your food thoroughly. This gives the food a better chance of being digested as much as possible in your mouth, so your stomach has an easier time of it.

- Caffeine, alcohol and tobacco should be avoided or reduced for a healthy, happy tummy.

- If all else fails, consider the FODMAP diet, which stands for Fermentable Oligosaccharides, Disaccharides, Monosaccharides and Polyols. It is almost as hard to stick to as it is to pronounce, but it seems to be very helpful for some people. A clinical study found that 86 per cent of subjects noticed improvements in their IBS symptoms.[12] The FODMAP diet basically entails cutting out foods such as apples, wheat, dairy and beans, which all contain types of carbohydrate that are easily fermented (read: gas-producing!) by your gut bacteria. But a word of caution: because it's such a restrictive diet it's recommended that you only follow it under the guidance of a dietician or nutritionist, rather than going it alone. You risk missing out on vital nutrients if you try to DIY.

Caffeine

While it's unlikely that caffeine is the root cause of your anxiety, it could well be making things worse. Anyone who's ever hit the espressos too hard or had one Red Bull too many on a night out will have experienced its jittery-making effects. The thing with caffeine is that, if you overdo it, the symptoms feel a lot like anxiety. Too many coffees can make you feel nauseous, nervous, give you a racing heartbeat and make it hard to focus, all of which can create a vicious cycle for more anxiety.

One of the reasons for this is that caffeine ramps up the production of adrenaline and cortisol. In one study, it doubled the levels of stress in the participants' hormones.[13] It also reduces the effects of your friend GABA, which you may remember from the previous chapter as the calming neurotransmitter.[14] One study found that high doses of caffeine produce a panic attack in 60 per cent of participants who already suffered from a panic disorder, and in 16 per cent of those with social anxiety – compared with none of the control group. Bad news for stressy coffee lovers![15] And if you have trouble sleeping, caffeine could be at least in part to blame. According to the American Academy of Sleep Medicine, caffeine stays active in your body for between eight and fourteen hours. So, is it time to find a different mid-morning and/or mid-afternoon pick-me-up?

The reason too much caffeine is not good for you on

both a mental and physical level is that it stresses your adrenal glands. These are two tiny, triangle-shaped glands that sit atop your kidneys and their job is to regulate your stress hormones, such as cortisol and adrenaline. Too much caffeine creates a low-level stress response in the body, meaning the adrenals have to work harder.

While caffeine definitely can be a problem for the anxious among us, there are too many variables to say for sure that it affects everyone in the same way or to the same extent. The only way to find out how it affects you is to test it for yourself. Try cutting down or cutting out coffee, tea and any other source of caffeine such as energy drinks or colas, and make a note of how you feel. It might be that there's a sweet spot – say, having just one coffee a day – so that you can still enjoy a daily cuppa without upsetting your adrenal glands.

A word of warning: caffeine withdrawal can result in pretty terrible headaches (in my experience, anyway). It's testament to what a powerful drug it is. Make sure you have painkillers to hand and plenty of decaf – or plain water, which is even better – to help you stay hydrated. Withdrawal usually only lasts a few days, so hang in there. And long term, some stimulant-free alternatives that I like are rooibos tea, hot water with a slice of lemon, barley or chicory coffee alternatives, or for a serious anti-inflammatory boost, a turmeric latte (find a recipe at calmer-you.com/turmeric-latte).

Alcohol

If you'd told the eighteen-year-old me that one day I would spend a year as a non-drinker I would have laughed so hard I probably would have spat my vodka and Coke in your face. Back then, alcohol was my great enabler, taking me from being shy around new people to the life and soul of the party in a few short sips. I bonded with new friends, had the courage to meet boys and survived working late nights in a bar, all with alcohol as my constant companion. Alcohol helped me lose my inhibitions so that I finally felt free to be 'me' (albeit a drunken me) in all sorts of new situations. Fears faded into the background and I could temporarily forget about my worries and relax. It was a revelation . . . for a while.

Alcohol felt like part of my identity as a teenager and early-twenty-something. I would pride myself on the number of snakebite and blacks I could consume on a night out, and I lived for Fridays. (For the uninitiated, snakebite and black is a horrible drink made of half cider, half beer, topped up with blackcurrant cordial.) But while drinking seemed to help at the time, the following day was a disaster. At uni my friends and I called it 'alcohol anxiety' – that horrible feeling the day after the night before when you're riddled with angst, guilt and worry. Wondering what embarrassing things you said or did, feeling guilty about the money you pissed away, fixating on that pain behind your eyes that you're sure isn't simply a headache.

For many of us, our lives are tied up with drinking. It's the nation's favourite pastime. It's been normalized to the point that if you don't drink, you're in the slim minority and often mocked. If you suffer from anxiety, alcohol can feel like the (temporary) answer to all your problems. It provides relief from having to think about the situation that's making you anxious and creates a shield of liquid confidence to hide behind. We use it to numb our pain and fears, but as with all numbing activities, the problem still bubbles away below the surface.

In 2014, during a health and wellbeing kick, I embarked on a year-and-a-half-long stint of booze-free living. I realized that, without alcohol to hide behind, I would have to learn how to bring my confidence up a level and create an authentic feeling of being comfortable in my own skin, especially when out in the evenings. No more supping a glass of 'Cab Sav' to ease a worried mind or a G&T to lubricate a networking event. Those eighteen months taught me so much. I felt physically better in every way, more energized, more inspired, and I learnt I could be confident in situations without alcohol.

There were certainly times – a friend's wedding, for example – when I would have loved to celebrate with a glass of champagne. But I was almost always able to still enjoy myself, and I had a great time at my best friend's hen do, dancing to eighties music until 3 a.m., stone cold sober! There was no more day-after guilt, and gone were any anxiety-triggering, hangover-induced body sensations to misinterpret as something more sinister.

Although I may have 'missed out' on some fun, if I had been drinking I would have missed out on even more: all the good feelings, calmness and opportunities that came because I was more myself and, well, healthier. If you close one door, another opens, as they say, and I found life had a way of bringing good things to me to fill the space that used to be taken up with drinking. These days, I drink every now and again, but I feel I've 'reset' my drinking so I don't have to have a drink to be comfortable in tricky social situations or to have fun.

I'm not suggesting you necessarily need to go all out and become a teetotaller, but explore for yourself whether cutting alcohol out or cutting down could be right for you. When you stop numbing yourself you open up to allowing more growth and progress. It might be uncomfortable at first, but you absolutely can handle it and the results will be so worth it.

. . . .

Exercise: the 'drink less' experiment

Draw two columns on a piece of paper. Consider the pros and cons of drinking and weigh them up. What benefits do you get from alcohol? Does it help you feel calmer at parties? Or switch off your overthinking brain for a while? How does it harm you or hold you back? Perhaps you feel panicky and nervous the day after, or Mondays are an anxious nightmare after a weekend on the booze? Looking at the good and bad points of drinking can help you make a decision about whether cutting down is right for you.

· ·

Try cutting out alcohol for two weeks and see what effect it has on you. The results may motivate you to do it longer term.

If other people object to you not drinking – maybe they think you're a party pooper, or that you look down on them for drinking – be strong in your decision and explain *why* you're doing it. Or, if that's too difficult, just make something up. Pretend you're on medication or that you drove into town. Remember, any issues they have with you not drinking are *their* stuff and not about you.

Have an alcohol action plan to help you stay on track. You could try alternating soft drinks with alcoholic ones, or just have two drinks before heading home. And it might sound overly simple, but ordering something that is not particularly delicious can mean you drink less. It's far easier to moderate how much you drink when it's plain old vodka sodas rather than yummy Martinis.

Sugar

When I talk to people about which foods negatively impact their anxiety, the one that comes up again and again is sugar. The problem with the sweet stuff (and with processed carbs such as white bread, white rice, pasta and potatoes, all of which break down fast in the body into their constituent sugars) is that it rapidly raises our blood sugar levels, which can in turn give us a rush of energy. This is all well and good, until the inevitable crash that leaves us light-headed, weak, shaky and unable to concentrate – all of which feels similar to anxiety. For some people, a sugar crash is virtually indistinguishable from the beginnings of a panic attack. Not nice. Those unpleasant feelings can have us reaching for more sugary stuff, and so the cycle continues. It's these ups and downs that are the problem; it's always better to be on an even keel when it comes to our minds and bodies, right?

Sugar and refined carbs might also contribute to inflammation, which, as we've already seen, is bad news for the brain and exacerbates anxiety.

The answer to all of this? Try to keep your blood-sugar levels steady. If you're having a sugar crash, reach for a banana and some nuts instead of toast or biscuits. You don't need to cut all the carbs from your diet and there's no need to see sugar as the enemy. After all, most of us like a sweet treat every now and again. But reducing the overall amount of sugar in your diet could help to keep you feeling more balanced in terms of energy and mood.

Tips for balancing blood-sugar levels

- Choose slow-release carbohydrates such as wholemeal bread and pasta, brown rice, quinoa and buckwheat.
- Consuming protein with your carbs will help to slow the absorption of sugar into your blood. Have some chicken, fish or egg with your rice or potatoes, a handful of nuts along with your fruit, and some meat or fish with your pasta. Vegans could have beans, lentils or tofu with their carbohydrates.
- There is some evidence[16] that cinnamon can help to steady blood-glucose levels. I'm not suggesting you can beat anxiety simply by loading up on this sweet spice, especially not in the form of iced cinnamon buns (although that would be awesome if it worked!), but you could sprinkle half a teaspoon on your bowl of apple crumble to mitigate some of the sugar's effects.
- Keep a healthy snack with you at all times so that if you feel your blood-sugar levels start to dip and your energy wane, you'll have something good to hand rather than grabbing a choccy bar that will leave you feeling lethargic again after about thirty minutes. Nuts and fruit, veg sticks and houmous, boiled eggs, Greek yoghurt, a spoonful or sachet of nut butter, or a chicken-salad wrap could all work well.

Supplements

There's no such thing as a cure for anxiety in the form of a pill, and taking supplements should never be an alternative to eating a healthy diet. Not everyone needs to take supplements, but it's definitely worth considering some of these, depending on your symptoms and diet. It's also a good idea to speak to your doctor before you start on supplements since, sometimes, they can interact with any medication you might be taking.

Magnesium

This is sometimes called the relaxation mineral because it helps your muscles relax (which is why it's found in many bath salts). Since the soil our food is grown in is often lacking in minerals, including magnesium, many of us are now deficient. And if you're anxious, you might be particularly short of it.

Studies have found that being stressed or anxious depletes our bodies of magnesium, while supplementation appears to protect us against the effects of stress.[17]

What's more, a 2010 study found that magnesium, when taken with vitamin B6 in a supplement, reduced the symptoms of premenstrual syndrome, including anxiety and mood changes.[18] So it's worth a shot, right? Magnesium is also anti-inflammatory and stimulates the calming neurotransmitter GABA's receptors. It's an amazing multitasker!

Great sources of magnesium include wholegrain wheat and brown rice, beans, nuts and good old dark green leafy veggies. Don't fancy popping a magnesium pill or chowing down on a ton of kale? Why not have a soak in the bath instead. Put 100–200g of Epsom salts or, even better, magnesium flakes (try the ones by Better You) into a warm bath and soak for twenty minutes. The magnesium-rich salts are absorbed through your skin, helping your muscles to relax. If you don't have time for a full-body soak, you could do a quick foot bath (my personal fave) while you sit on the couch and chill.

Vitamin D

According to the NHS, between October and early March us folks in the UK won't be receiving any vitamin D from sunlight because it simply isn't strong enough (need we be reminded!). We get some vitamin D from our food – oily fish, eggs and red meat – but we're only ever able to extract a small proportion of our needs that way. Basically, we need exposure to the sun. When the UV rays hit our skin they cause our bodies to produce the vitamin (which is actually a hormone, but I won't go into that as it's way too technical!). A shortage of vitamin D is one of the most common deficiencies in the UK and most of us would do well to take a supplement.

Numerous studies have found a link between vitamin D levels and mental health. In one, people with anxiety were found to have lower levels of vitamin D in their bodies than the control participants.[19] Another study found that patients who took a vitamin D supplement had an increase in their levels of wellbeing and fewer depressive symptoms.[20] A large study in 2013 found a link between low vitamin D levels and panic disorders, too.[21]

It used to be thought that having fifteen to thirty minutes of exposure to the sun, three to four times a week during the summer months would give you enough vitamin D to last almost through the winter. These days, the NHS recommends that everyone takes a vitamin D supplement of 10mcg a day, although it may not be necessary in the summer months if you are getting enough sunlight. And if you have dark skin, which doesn't absorb as much UV, or you're not much of a sun seeker, it's particularly important to take your supplement.

Omega-3

Read the ingredients on any processed-food package and you'll likely see fats such as sunflower oil, corn oil, peanut oil or soybean oil. All of these are plant oils and you'd think a plant-based oil would be healthy, right? Wrong. While these fats aren't harmful in small amounts they are added to so many processed foods that we end up consuming too much of them. They're cheap, tasteless and the food industry loves to stick 'em in everything from biscuits to takeaways. These oils are high in omega-6 fats so most of us are getting too much 6 and not enough omega-3.

Our brains are made up of around 60 per cent fat. Ideally, omega-3 fats would be used to make up the walls of brain cells but eating a diet high in processed foods means that we end up with omega-6 rather than 3 in our brains. Omega-6 causes inflammation, making brain cells less flexible and impairing the signalling between them.

First things first: in order to reduce the amount of omega-6 fat in your body, try to limit the amount of processed food you eat. Then you need to boost your consumption of omega-3 fats. The NHS recommends we eat at least one portion of oily fish a week. This could be salmon, fresh tuna (tinned doesn't count, sadly, as the omega oils are under the skin), mackerel or sardines. You might also want to consider taking a supplement of fish or krill, which is a type of teeny, tiny shrimp that larger fish live off. For vegetarians, an omega-3 supplement made of flax seeds or algae oil is worth considering.

Summary

★ Your diet doesn't need to be yet another source of stress. Food is not the enemy and small changes, which can have a big positive impact on your anxiety levels, are better and more sustainable than extreme measures.

cont.

★ Eating quickly or in a stressed state makes it more difficult for your digestive system to function. Slow down, and stop multitasking when you eat!

★ A great anti-anxiety diet limits sugar, caffeine and alcohol.

★ Eat plenty of anti-inflammatory foods such as green leafy veg, broccoli, oily fish and dark berries. Avoid pro-inflammatory fried foods, processed meats and sugar.

★ Eat mindfully by savouring every bite, and try to see your food as an aspect of self-care: eat like you love yourself.

★ Most importantly, enjoy your food!

CHAPTER 9

The Anxiety Solution Toolkit

Worry never robs tomorrow of its sorrow, it
only saps today of its joy.

LEO BUSCAGLIA

This chapter contains a whole host of practical ways you
can minimize your anxiety. It's impossible to stamp out
all worry completely, but the following techniques have
helped me and countless of my clients reduce their
mountain of anxiety to an insignificant molehill. They
can help you, too, if you incorporate them into each day.

At the end of the chapter is a section called Trigger
tables. A trigger is anything that causes you to feel anxious.
I've given some examples of common triggers, along
with suggestions for how to manage them. It can be really
helpful to track your own triggers and make a plan for
how to handle them. And the final section of the chapter
is a question-and-answer session (Q&A) based on the
scenarios I see most frequently with my clients.

Not all the exercises I suggest will chime equally with
you. That's fine. We're all different. But I would urge you
to try all of them once; you never know how you're going

to get on with a technique until you try it. I can't tell you how many times a client has said to me something along the lines of 'I don't do affirmations, they just seem so silly,' only to come back a month later reporting that they wouldn't miss saying their daily affirmations in front of the bathroom mirror for the world. Keep an open mind and remember, some of these techniques take a bit of practise. As always, you don't have to be perfect at any of them, and certainly not straight away.

Let's start with perhaps the most transformative of them all (though it's not always easy to do . . .).

Schedule your 'worry time'

One of the worst things about worrying is that it invades your everyday life. It sours moments that should be happy; it keeps you awake when you could be having much-needed brain-repairing beauty sleep; and it takes up mental and emotional bandwidth that I know you'd much rather be spending elsewhere.

So, let me introduce you to the concept of 'worry time'. That's right, folks, a designated time slot into which you pour all your worries and keep them tightly contained there. It's what psychotherapist and author of *The Worry Cure: Stop Worrying and Start Living*, Dr Robert Leahy, suggests you do for twenty minutes each day. If you find yourself worrying at any other time, you write the worry down and postpone thinking about it until your allocated worry slot. This helps to eliminate one of the worst types of worry, which is meta-worry (that is, worrying about worrying). Having a system in place means meta-worry becomes a thing of the past. It might not be easy to postpone fretting at first, but worry is just a habit, and the more you get into the new habit, the easier it will be.

• •

Exercise: scheduling worry time

Choose a time when you know you'll be alone for a while. Worry time works better if you can do it at the same moment each day, as that helps form a habit – perhaps just after dinner, or on your way home from work if you don't drive.

Get a pad of paper and a pen and write down all the things you're worried about. You could do this on your phone but pen and paper feels more solid and cathartic. Now, notice which of these are things you have some control over and which are outside your influence. If there are things you *do* have some control over, find a way to take action right now. Worry, after all, can be a way of avoiding having to deal with things. So, for each worry, ask yourself, 'What action can I take right now?' If there is no obvious immediate action, can you at least make a plan? Jot down the first three steps of your plan and schedule them. Once you take action or start making plans, you'll feel more effective, more focused.

• •

This technique really helped me a few years ago, when I was worried about money. I had just become self-employed and business was slow. I found myself getting caught up with worries about not having enough cash. A lot of my time was taken up with worries that just seemed to go in circles. I realized I had to take action, so I made a list of income-producing ideas. Then I drew up a budget, mapping out what my outgoings would be over the next few months. Doing this gave me back a sense of control, helped me to feel constructive and put my mind at ease.

As you get into the habit of writing down your worries you'll start to notice patterns in the types of things that create anxiety for you. You'll probably notice that you have a lot of the same circular worries again and again. This will show you where to concentrate your 'worry time' efforts.

But what about the things that are out of our control? I hear you ask. The worries for which it would be impossible to take action or make a plan, such as worrying obsessively about other people's welfare? These still need to be written down. Worries can seem nightmarish if left to circle your brain unfettered. Writing down those out-of-your-control thoughts will help you get them into perspective.

• •

Exercise: writing down all worries, unedited

Stream-of-consciousness writing is an effective way to help you empty your head of worries and to uncover the real fears often hidden below the surface anxiety.

- Grab your paper or notebook and begin to write about something that's troubling you. Keep going for at least five minutes. Don't stop; let your hand scribble down anything your brain throws up. Sometimes writing it down can be enough to calm you.
- If that doesn't help things to shift, try 'answering back' to the worry. Imagine what your best friend, your mum, a judge, or even a celeb you look up to, such as Beyoncé would say about your worry. How might they see things differently from you? What kind or encouraging words would they offer? How would they put things into perspective for you? Practise 'answering back' to your worries.
- As an example, say I'm worried about my boyfriend injuring himself on his snowboarding holiday. This is clearly something outside my control and aside, from telling him to be careful, there's not much in the way of action I can take. So I might write down what my best friend would say about this. In a very patient and loving way she would point out that the chances of him having

163

a serious injury are very small, that he's a careful person and that everything will be OK. She would remind me that I am just 'thinking the worst' and that the *probability* of him injuring himself was very small. Beyoncé would likely tell me to focus on my own career and stop fretting over a guy, and a judge would say that, though it's pointless to worry about something so unlikely to happen, even if it *did*, I should remember that I am an infinitely resourceful and capable person. I can handle it.

- It takes practice, but each time you reframe things in this way you are creating new neural pathways in your brain that make it easier to think positively in the future.

. . . .

Do a social media cleanse

As we've seen in previous chapters, social media and limitless Internet use can be a factor in our increasing anxiety. Obsessive Instagram and Facebook habits lead to 'comparisonitis' and feed low self-esteem. Too much time online can also make us feel overwhelmed by being available 24/7. It's not all bad, of course, but if it affects you negatively, consider doing the following . . .

- Enforce a 'no-email zone' between 9 p.m. and 9 a.m. – or choose hours to suit your life. You'll be more able to switch off your brain at night and will have a more chilled-out morning. Now that I check my phone later in the day, my head is clearer and I can enjoy my morning, free of distractions and potential stress.

- Figure out what your triggers are. Do certain news sites whip you into a worried frenzy about the state of the world? Does that yoga woman on Instagram give you unbearable FOMO? Consider just not visiting the sites or apps that drive you crazy, or at least curate what you look at. It *is* possible to block sites on your Internet browser or un-follow certain people, you know! If someone posts stuff that drags you down, be kind to yourself and un-follow them, at least until you're in a better mental place. Treat yourself like an experiment: if ditching news sites and social media for a week makes you feel lighter and freer, you could be on to something.

- Have an SOS: Switch-off Sunday. This means unplugging for the *whole day*. Leave your phone off, unhook the Wi-Fi and enjoy a day of blissful, undisturbed peace. Go outside if you can, and fully connect to the real world around you, not the online, digitally enhanced version.

Try meditation – your daily chill pill

Think of meditation as the ultimate 'me time'. No distractions, nothing else to do but focus on doing something really amazing for yourself. We all need that. And if you're anxious, I'd say meditation is essential. Taking time for yourself is not selfish; in fact, it's the best thing you can do for everyone in your life. We all need time to recharge and it will make you a better friend, partner, mother, girlfriend, sister, daughter, employee or business owner and general human being as a result!

If you've got some resistance towards meditation, notice what thoughts pop up about it. Are you telling yourself there's no time, or that you can't switch off enough to meditate, or that it's too airy-fairy? Question these thoughts and ask yourself, 'Is this really true?' Sometimes we resist things because, deep down, we know that they might help, and change can be scary. Consider that if you're really resistant to something, it might be because it's something that will truly help you.

If you're convinced you have no time to meditate, for example, I would challenge you to think about how you are prioritizing your time. I'll always remember watching an interview with Beyoncé where she talked about how she once put oven chips into a deep-fat fryer and practically caused a house fire. She'd never learnt to cook. That's probably because she'd been prioritizing other things such as practising until she was an amazing singer, and building her empire!

We all have the same twenty-four hours in a day and we can choose how we spend at least some of that time. Sometimes it can feel as if there are a million demands on you and your time is not your own, but you have more choices than you think. And fundamentally, if you're waiting for more time to materialize to do your meditation or take care of yourself, you're going to be waiting for ever! You've got to make the time. It's all about priorities.

I've been known to spend five minutes that turned into an hour getting drawn into some celebrity gossip site that only makes me feel crap anyway. Eventually, I realized it was because I wanted to do something *mindless* that would help me to switch my brain off. These days, I try to use my chill-out time more wisely, by meditating and being *mindful*.

Look at what you're doing to unwind and ask yourself, 'Is it really working, and is there a better way to spend that time?' Whether you've been playing Candy Crush, reading junk online or aimlessly cruising social media, could you use that time to really relax and do something positive for yourself? The truth is, we all have ten minutes a day to meditate; we just need to choose to do it rather than doing something else.

Meditating first thing in the morning works for lots of people. Katy Perry props herself up in bed as soon as she wakes and does twenty minutes of transcendental meditation, a type of meditation where you say a mantra silently to yourself. 'It puts me in the best mood. It's the only time my brain gets complete rest.'[1] As Katy says, 'I don't have a whole lot of time. Meditation extends my day so I can live at my fullest capacity.' Think of it as an investment of your time that pays back in happiness, calmness, focus and productivity many times over.

So when is a good moment to meditate?

- If you commute to work by train or bus, make the most of that time by closing your eyes and listening to a guided meditation or mindfulness meditation.
- Or why not sit in the park at lunchtime and take ten minutes for yourself?
- You could also meditate as soon as you get home from work, to wash away the day's stress.
- Another time is right before bed, although you might be too tired by then, so it doesn't work for everyone. Try it. If you keep falling asleep, another time in the day might be better.

If you're telling yourself you won't be any good at meditation, try to take a step back from your perfectionist worry. It's all too easy to put a ton of pressure on yourself to be brilliant at everything and, if you generally need things to be perfect then you'll probably be the same with meditation. You'll convince yourself that, unless you can clear your mind of all the internal chatter or sit cross-legged like a Zen monk for hours, then it's just not worth bothering. 'I knew there was something there for me, in meditation, but every time I would try to do it, I was like, "I just cannot meditate!"' Cameron Diaz once said in an interview.[2] She stuck with it, though, and now she is a spokesperson for the benefits of meditation. What helped me the most was being very gentle with myself, resisting my need for the meditation to be a certain way and instead just going through the process.

Different types of meditation

There are lots of types of meditation, and different styles will work for different people. If you've tried one type before and didn't get on with it, don't give up! We can all meditate; it's just about finding something that suits us.

Mindfulness meditation

This involves paying very close attention to your breath. It trains your mind to be in the present moment, which is so helpful for relieving anxiety. One study found that mindfulness meditation helped to reduce activity in the amygdala – the part of the brain responsible for feeling fear[3] while in another, mindfulness helped 90 per cent of people reduce their anxiety levels.[4] When you're mindful, present and aware, you're much less likely to spin off into negative thinking or worries, and that can only be a good thing.

Something I find fascinating is how meditation actually changes the structure of your brain – in a good way! Neuroscientist Sara Lazar at Massachusetts General

Hospital and Harvard Medical School carried out research with long-term meditators. Participants doing mindfulness meditation showed a reduction in the sizes of their amygdalas and Sara concluded that they consequently had less of a tendency to overreact to perceived threats. They felt less stressed and anxious and became more self-aware and able to better navigate potentially stressful events.[5]

I hope you're convinced of the benefits and raring to go! Start with the following simple meditation exercise. You can also try the Anxiety Solution mindfulness meditation download in the online book bonuses, or one of many commercial apps available. If you fancy going to a class or getting some guidance in person, you could also check out your local Buddhist centre. When I went to mine, there were all sorts of people there and it didn't feel in any way religious; there were builders, bankers, students, mums, old folks, young hipsters, media luvvies and every type of person in between.

· ·

Exercise: mindfulness meditation

- Set a timer for fifteen minutes. If possible, find a timer app with a gentle gong sound that you can programme to go off at five-minute intervals. Sit comfortably (it doesn't have to be on the floor, or cross-legged), with your hands facing upwards on your lap, eyes closed.

- Inhale and exhale normally, focusing on the sensation of the air passing into and out of your nostrils.
- For the first five minutes, silently count up to ten after the exhales. In other words, after each complete inhale and exhale, count 'one' in your head, then after the next one, count 'two'. Do this all the way up to ten, though don't be surprised if you don't get anywhere close to ten before your mind has wandered off down some thought trail.
- As soon as you notice your mind has wandered, gently bring it back to the breath, starting at one again.
- After five minutes, change the count so it's before the inhales. Although, technically, it's the same thing, changing where you place the count emphasizes the inhale more than the exhale, making it subtly different.
- Continue for another five minutes, this time losing the count and focusing purely on the sensation of the breath going into and out of your nostrils, throat and lungs. Immerse yourself in this sensation until the timer goes off.

· ·

Transcendental meditation

This type of meditation, often abbreviated to TM, involves silently repeating a mantra (a sound or word) to yourself as you sit with your eyes closed. The mantra is given to you by a practitioner and is unique to you. Transcendental meditation helps to quieten the mind and lower stress. Evidence shows that it reduces anxiety more effectively than pure relaxation techniques[6] and reduces levels of stress hormones.[7] It's also thought that TM helps to strengthen communication between the brain's prefrontal cortex and other areas, which means that emotional responses to life are more balanced.[8] TM needs to be learnt from a qualified teacher so, to find out more, visit uk.tm.org.

Guided meditation

This involves the participant listening to instructions on how to think in a focused way about certain things, such as a nature scene; or parts of the body, in order to relax them. Guided meditation, which some say is more visualization than pure meditation, has been found to induce the 'relaxation response' by lowering heart rate and reducing blood pressure.[9]

Guided meditation practice has also been found to significantly reduce perceived stress levels. Get a free guided meditation in the online book bonuses section at www.calmer-you.com/bonus.

. . . .

Exercise: guided visualization meditation

Sit comfortably in a chair, or lie down in bed, and close your eyes. Take some deep breaths through your nose. With each out breath, feel yourself settling further into your seat or on to the bed. Then either say the following words slowly to yourself in your own mind, or record them on your phone to play back to yourself. Remember to pause between each sentence to give yourself time to engage your imagination. If you're not a visual person, tune into the sounds or feelings instead.

Imagine you are walking along a beautiful, peaceful beach. Imagine smelling the sea air and feeling the sand underfoot. As you take each step, you feel more and more comfortable. Feel the warm sun on your skin and hear the sound of waves rolling into the shore. Look around and notice the blue sky and the sunshine sparkling on the surface of the ocean. As you walk along the shore, the cool, refreshing water laps over your feet, washing away stress as each wave recedes. You continue to walk along the beach, noticing everything you see, hear, smell and feel and allowing every step to relax you more and more.

. . . .

Moving meditation

If a seated meditation seems impossible to you right now, try one that involves movement. Practising yoga, doing t'ai chi or even walking can all be forms of meditation when you pay very close attention to what you're doing. The next time you go for a walk, read the following meditation a couple of times first and then use it to guide and focus your thoughts when you're out.

• •

Exercise: a simple walking meditation

Notice the feeling of the ground under your feet, the air on your skin and the sights, sounds and smells around you. Pay close attention to every step and the feeling of your body as it moves. Notice all the subtle sensations of your feet touching and then leaving the ground as you walk. As soon as you notice your attention wandering off, as it *always* will, bring it back to the experience of walking. A wandering mind is totally natural, so don't worry about it, just keep bringing your attention back to the feeling of walking. It's a great way to calm you mentally and help you to be more present.

• •

Be mindful in the moment

Mindfulness has been in the media a lot over the past five years or so and it kind of goes hand in hand with meditation. If you meditate, you're naturally going to be more mindful, but you don't necessarily need to meditate every day to make mindfulness a part of your life.

The essence of mindfulness is to pay attention to the present moment rather than worrying about stuff from the past or in the future. It's also about being open to your current thoughts and feelings rather than judging yourself for having them or trying to control or suppress them. Mindfulness helps you to be the objective observer of your thoughts rather than getting tangled up with and pulled down by them. Being the observer means recognizing you are *not* your thoughts but rather the *awareness of* your thoughts. I view mindfulness as a workout for my brain. Your attention is like a muscle, and the more you flex it, the stronger it gets and the calmer and happier you become as a result.

This awareness of our thoughts is vital because our thoughts both reflect and determine our moods. Although it's almost impossible to measure, it's often estimated that we have between 12,000 and 70,000 thoughts every day. A sad fact is that the vast majority of this mental chatter is negative. Psychologists call it 'negativity dominance'. In a study by Dr Raj Raghunathan at the University of Texas, students were asked to record their automatic thoughts throughout the day. It was found that 60–70 per cent of these thoughts were negative. The problem is, negative thinking becomes a habit. It's believed that 98 per cent of our thoughts are in the same mood as the ones we had yesterday.[10] Left unchecked, those negative thoughts can quickly turn into a habitual bad or anxious mood that feels as if it's an inevitable part of our life and personality. So it's vital to disrupt the obsessive negative thinking. When you're more mindful, if a negative thought does pop in, such as 'I'll never be good enough to get promoted' or 'I'm a terrible mum,' you will be able to see it for what it is – just a passing thought – rather than taking it too seriously. It's a bit like standing on the ground looking up at clouds. When you're not being mindful, you can get sucked up into a tornado if you're not careful! Being mindful means you can observe the clouds as they float overhead and then out of sight.

Mindfulness is fantastic for tackling habitual negativity and it's also a powerful weapon against the mindless churn of worry that can make you feel as if you're living on autopilot. A few months ago I was walking along a street and had something on my mind. It wasn't until I reached my destination that I realized I'd been on total autopilot the whole way there and had no recollection of seeing anything between points A and B. I had been mulling over some possible outcomes for a work situation and replaying stressful conversations I'd had in the past. I hadn't even noticed I was worrying. Worry had hijacked the controls and I was just along for the unhappy ride. I used to do this *all* the time.

When our minds are on autopilot, we're not really in control of the thoughts that pop up. Any old rubbish can come in because, unfortunately, thanks to negativity dominance, our minds often gravitate towards negative thoughts and worries. Mindfulness increases your awareness of your whole environment, including the thoughts you're thinking. It puts you back in control of what you think about and sets you on course to a better mood and less anxiety.

Mindfulness is also an immunization against overthinking. When we're more mindful and present, we're not getting lost down the rubbish chute of worry. It's impossible to be mindful of the present moment and to worry about the future at the same time. Your brain literally can't do those two things at once. So, as often as I can, when I'm walking to work, I tune into the colour of the sky and the patterns of the clouds. I notice the feeling of the ground underfoot, the breeze on my skin, and the smells and sounds around me. It's like being 'at the controls' of my mind rather than on auto-pilot. If a negative thought comes in, it's easier for me to catch it before it spirals. I'm able to recognize that the thought is just a thought, not a fact. I become the observer of my mind rather than believing I am the thoughts themselves.

Mindfulness meditation, where you 'watch your breath', is a great way to flex your mindfulness muscles, but it's not the only one. Here are some simple things you can do to add more mindfulness to your life without having to sit on a cushion for twenty minutes.

In the shower

As you lather up your body and shampoo your hair, pay attention to the feel of the water, the smell of the soap and the sensation of massaging your scalp. I used to worry and stress about the day ahead while I was showering, but these days I use it as time to be present and tune into the moment.

As you eat

Step away from emails at lunchtime and instead focus entirely on what you are eating. Most of us rush through our food and barely even taste it. Why not use meal times as a chance to practise being mindful? Notice the colours and smells of your food, eat slowly and pay attention to each bite.

While you clean

Yes, folks, who knew that doing the washing-up could be an antidote to anxiety? When you're totally focused on scrubbing those plates, feeling the suds and the warmth of the water and smelling the washing-up liquid, you can't be worrying at the same time. Plus, there's something strangely satisfying about being really present as you do housework. I'm serious! Try it.

During a workout

It's easy to want to mentally 'check out' when you exercise (I know I'm not the only one who wants to avoid feeling the burn!), but being mindful as you run, swim or do yoga can deliver rewards that go way beyond the physical. Use this time to tune into your body and your surroundings and to tone your mindfulness muscle as well as your glutes. This is even more powerful when you exercise outside rather than staring at the wall in front of you while you pound the treadmill. It's just more inspiring to lose yourself in nature and the natural environment.

A quick zapper for negative thoughts

This very simple tool is extremely effective. Every time you catch yourself getting caught up in negative internal chatter, address the negative thought directly. Hear it out and then say, 'Thanks for sharing.' Acknowledging the thought is easier than trying not to hear it in the first place. When you thank it for its contribution, you recognize the part of you that is anxiously trying to keep you safe, even if it's completely misguided and its approach isn't very friendly! When you say, 'Thanks for sharing,' you can kiss your negative thoughts goodbye.

Part of the reason this technique is so powerful is that it builds on the fact that you are not your thoughts, which is a fundamental insight derived from mindfulness. Once you learn to step back and observe your thoughts, you are back in the driving seat.

So if these thoughts are not 'you', where are they coming from? Often they bubble up automatically from your subconscious mind, the result of things you've been told and beliefs you have about yourself and the world. They are like mental reflexes, based on programming and experiences from the past.

When you were a child, you might have been told things such as 'The world is a dangerous place,' or 'Be a good girl so your teacher will like you.' When you're young, your brain is like a sponge. It soaks up anything and everything, and of course you lack the life experience to evaluate the validity or usefulness of the things you hear. Naturally, you end up believing many of them. These beliefs tend to hang around and colour your thoughts, feelings and habits. They are often untrue, but that doesn't stop your subconscious mind from replaying them again and again.

I had a client, Sara, who as a child was told by her stepfather that she wasn't intelligent. Her subconscious mind replayed this belief over and over with thoughts such as, 'I'm too stupid to speak in public,' and 'There's no point going for the promotion, I'll never be good enough.' Despite the fact that she had a PhD, she worried constantly that she was a fraud. I suggested to her that she try out the negative thought zapper. It took a bit of practice but eventually Sara learnt to say to the thought, 'Thanks for sharing,' and then ignore it.

Be grateful for the good stuff

I've had client after client tell me that practising gratitude is the thing that helps them shift from a negative to a positive mindset almost instantly. It's another one of those seriously simple but mega-powerful ideas that really works.

When we're anxious, we're prone to thinking the worst and focusing on the negative stuff. But what if you could rewire your brain to be more optimistic? In his book *The Happiness Advantage: The Seven Principles of Positive Psychology that Fuel Success and Performance at Work*, psychologist Shawn Achor describes how being grateful for the good things in our lives and mentally 'seeking out' more of them trains our brains to see them automatically. It's like training a positivity muscle. People who actively look for the good and are thankful for it become more naturally optimistic and positive. There is solid evidence from numerous studies that regular gratitude practice improves mental wellbeing and makes us happier and calmer.[11]

· ·

Exercise: **practising gratitude daily**

Write down at least three specific things you're currently feeling grateful for. It might be something small such as the delicious cup of coffee you're drinking or having a beautiful park or garden to visit near where you live. Maybe it's the fact that your partner gives the best back rubs, or that an amazing bookshop has just opened up near your office.

The more specific you can be, the better, because it gives you more scope to think of new things each time you do the exercise and means you do more mental searching. If you just write 'I'm grateful for my family' every day, it's going to lose its meaning pretty fast, whereas if you list a different specific thing about each family member, this will work wonders!

Another powerful practice is to scan through the day just before you go to bed and make a note of all the things that went well. Perhaps you had a great catch-up with a colleague, or it was a nice day so you went for a walk, or you made a new recipe and it turned out great. Scanning the day for good things helps to make you feel more positive.

. . . .

Use affirmations to boost positivity

What have you been telling yourself recently? If you're anything like I used to be, chances are you've been a mental bully, locked in negative cycles of thinking, telling yourself that you're no good or will never feel better. The way we speak to ourselves is important. As a push back against all that self-critical chatter, I suggest creating some mantras or positive affirmations for yourself. When you repeat them, whether it's out loud, in your head or by writing them down, it starts to become a mental habit to think those positive thoughts. As we've already seen, thoughts can eventually become beliefs, through sheer repetition and force of habit.

Affirmations absolutely must be a positive statement, and they work best when you say them as if they are happening now. So instead of saying, 'I will never be scared of speaking in a meeting again,' or 'I will feel more confident,' tell yourself 'I am confident.' You can get a free affirmations audio track in the book bonuses section at www.calmer-you.com/bonus.

• •

Exercise: affirming positivity

Here are some examples you could use, or make up your own. Write them down and repeat them to yourself every day. You could stick them on Post-its around your home or make a note of them on your phone so you can refer to them easily. Say them like you mean them (even if you don't at first – that will come).

- I am confident
- I am relaxed and at ease
- I feel good about myself
- I am clear-headed and free
- I am enough
- My best is always good enough
- I am a kind person
- I am brave

✎ Write down your affirmations below:

....

....

....

....

....

....

....
....
....
....
....
....
....
....
....
....
....
....
....
....
. . . .

Practise self-compassion and self-love

Every single time you do something positive for yourself, such as cooking a healthy meal or sitting down to do a guided meditation, you are practising self-love. The basis of everything in this book is the idea that when you practise self-love it's an act of deep compassion towards yourself. And that's especially important for those of us who are prone to anxiety because so often we beat ourselves up, feeling guilty and being self-critical.

Self-compassion means forgiving yourself for petty errors and misdemeanours, the kind of things you would always overlook in a friend. Self-love, as we've already seen, is not about boosting your ego so much as caring for yourself as you would for a friend or family member who needed your help. In a way, this whole book is about self-love, but I want to share a couple of specific techniques to demonstrate to your deep self that you value yourself. They are guaranteed to put you in a better mood.

• •

Exercise: write yourself a letter of support

This first one comes from self-compassion researcher Dr Kristin Neff. The letter must be from the perspective of a friend who is unconditionally loving and accepting of you (it could be an imaginary friend). This friend knows you inside out, all your amazing qualities and all of your flaws, and accepts you totally. They recognize that, as a human being, you aren't perfect, nor should you be. You might want to write about their view of one of your current worries or something more general about you and the history of your friendship, but whatever you write about, fill the letter with understanding, support and love.

• •

. . . .

Exercise: **seeing through the eyes of someone who loves you**

Get comfortable and close your eyes. Imagine a person who really loves you is standing in front of you. Float up out of yourself and into their shoes. See yourself through their eyes. Feel with their heart. Hear with their ears. See all the incredible things that they see in you; your smile, your amazing sense of humour, your unique style, your beautiful mind and the quirks that make you the gorgeous, lovable woman that you are. From their perspective, tell yourself everything you need to know to understand how loved and valued you are. Send a warm glow back to yourself, then float back into yourself and receive it.

. . . .

Teach yourself to relax

If you've ever thought to yourself 'I can't relax,' or 'I can't switch off,' you're not alone. I hear it *all* the time. We get so used to being on high alert that we actually forget that being calm and at ease is our natural state. But relaxation is something that you can practise and get better at. Here are three simple ways to relax, wherever you are.

. . . .

Exercise: **the '3–5' breathing technique**

Put your hands on your belly and relax your stomach muscles. Take a deep breath in for a count of three and then breathe out for a count of five. As you breathe in, let your belly expand like a balloon, and as you breathe out, let the balloon, deflate. It doesn't matter how quickly or slowly you count; what's important is that the out breath is longer than the in breath and that you're breathing into your belly. What this breathing exercise does is send a message to your nervous system that it's safe to relax. Lengthening the out breath and breathing into our bellies gets us out of fight-or-flight mode and in to rest-and-digest (i.e. relaxation) mode. As an added bonus, focusing on counting helps to distract and calm your mind. Do it for a few minutes or for as long as you need to.

. . . .

Exercise: **the body-scan muscle relaxation**

The aim of this exercise is to mentally scan each part of your body, from your toes up to the top of your head, and consciously relax each muscle group. Begin by directing your attention to your toes and mentally say to yourself, 'Toes, relax.' Then move through your ankles, calves, knees, thighs, hips, stomach, buttocks, chest, back, shoulders, arms, hands, neck, scalp, forehead, eyes, mouth and jaw muscles. With each area, think, 'Relax,' or simply imagine the area relaxing. It's a great exercise for releasing tension from your body, calming your mind and bringing you in to the present moment.

. . . .

Exercise: tune into your body

It's basically impossible to be focused on your body while simultaneously worrying about something. You can't focus on the two at once, so tuning into how your body feels is a quick way to get out of your head. Whether you're sitting on the train, on the sofa or walking down the street, focus all your attention on how your body feels. Pay attention to the energy in your body, notice its temperature, notice the sensations or the feeling of your pulse. Try to allow the whole of your attention to be taken up by an awareness of what it feels like to be in your body. Hold it there for as long as you like. When your mind drifts, gently bring it back.

. . . .

Visualize your anxiety-free life

When you vividly imagine something, your unconscious mind doesn't know the difference between that and the real situation. Anyone who feels anxious just *thinking* about a fear-triggering situation will know this is true! Many people with anxiety use the power of their imagination to visualize the worst-case scenario, which only creates more angst. Instead, you can use your imagination as a force for good. When you mentally rehearse a situation that typically makes you anxious, imagining things turning out fine and handling any hiccups along the way all while remaining relaxed, you create new neural pathways in your brain that correspond with feeling relaxed when the real-life situation comes about. Sportspeople such as Usain Bolt and Michael Phelps are known to mentally rehearse their events. They see them going well in their minds and it helps them to be calm and confident in their competitions.

. . . .

Exercise: visualizing positivity

Close your eyes and get comfortable, lying in bed or sitting in a chair. Take some deep breaths and imagine your body settling further into the bed or chair with each out breath. Carry out the 'body-scan muscle relaxation', if you have time. Now begin to imagine a situation that has made you anxious in the past – examples might be giving a presentation, going to a new place, meeting new people or flying in an aeroplane. Tune into all your senses and visualize how you'll look, feel, behave, what you'll do and how other people will respond to you when you are next in the situation. Imagine what you'll hear and say and the

thoughts you'll have. Visualize yourself feeling confident, relaxed and comfortable. See that, if any problems
arise, you can handle them calmly. Imagine feeling
great afterwards, knowing that you did your best.

. . . .

Every time you do this exercise you are creating new
neural pathways which will eventually make these new
thoughts, feelings and behaviours automatic for you.
Practise this visualization daily for a few minutes and
you will train your brain to feel relaxed and confident in
the situation. Don't worry if you can't imagine things
clearly or you're not very visual, just do it in the best way
you can. Some people tune into the feelings rather than
the images, and that's just as good. Even if at first it
makes you anxious just to imagine a situation, mentally
rehearsing it will desensitize you to it. The process works
in the same way as classical conditioning (remember
Pavlov's dog?). Your brain learns to associate the scenario
with feeling relaxed instead of feeling fear. Keep practising until you feel completely calm when you think of the
situation.

. . . .

✎ Exercise: **Fill out the following tables to map out
how you will use your imagination to mentally
rehearse different situations. Using all your senses
helps to make it more powerful.**

The Anxiety Solution Toolkit

Example table:

Situation	Speaking up in a meeting
See	I imagine noticing how the meeting rooms looks. I make eye contact with the people I'm speaking with. I see people looking friendly and interested.
Feel	I feel grounded, calm and steady. The slight feeling of adrenaline is a sign that I'm excited about what I'm about to share.
Think	I have value to offer this meeting. The people in the meeting are rooting for me and want me to do well. I am focused on what I am saying.
Speak	I speak slowly and steadily, taking the time to pause and breathe. I speak clearly and articulately.
Hear	I hear people asking interested questions. My boss tells me how much they enjoyed my contribution.

Situation	
See	
Feel	
Think	
Speak	
Hear	

Situation	
See	
Feel	
Think	
Speak	
Hear	

Situation	
See	
Feel	
Think	
Speak	
Hear	

Situation	
See	
Feel	
Think	
Speak	
Hear	

Situation	
See	
Feel	
Think	
Speak	
Hear	

A checklist for better sleep

If anxiety prevents you from sleeping, ensure you've got the following ticked off to give yourself the best chance of a good night's rest.

- Caffeine hangs around in the body for hours after we drink it; some studies suggest for as long as fourteen hours. So keep coffee and tea drinking to the early mornings only.
- Reading fiction for twenty minutes or so before bed can help you to switch off and let go of the day. It's a great escape from your everyday life and worries.
- The bright blue lights from computers and phones stop our brains from producing melatonin, the chemical that makes us go to sleep. Stop using screens for at least an hour before bed and consider installing a program called Flux on your computer if you have to work late. It makes the light more orange-toned so that your brain still produces melatonin.
- Write yourself a to-do list for the following day so you don't have everything swirling around in your head as you're trying to drift off.
- Park your worries on paper before you go to bed. You can return to them in the morning, if you must!

- An obvious one, but do make sure your bedroom is dark enough or wear an eye mask. And block out any noise with headphones or earplugs.
- Try out the food supplement 5-HTP. It helps our bodies to produce serotonin and therefore makes us more relaxed and sleepy.
- Try a bit of pre-bedtime yoga, even if it's just a few gentle stretches. Check out Youtube for some instructional videos or try the app Yin Yoga if you don't already practise yoga.
- Do some 3–5 breathing. Breathe in for three and out for a count of five. It's all about lengthening the out breath, which reduces stress and gets the nervous system ready for sleep.
- Don't watch *Game of Thrones* (or any other 'exciting' programme) just before you go to bed, as it can amp you up too much to sleep. I've learnt this the hard way!

Trigger tables

A trigger is anything (an idea, a situation, a time of the year) that brings up anxious thoughts and feelings. It can be helpful to make a note of which situations trigger anxiety for you so that you can make a plan for how to handle that situation if it comes up again. Knowing that you're well prepared will help make the situation much easier to manage.

You may find that some of these examples resonate with you. The most valuable thing you can do, though, is to grab your notebook and draw up your own trigger tables, making them as specific and personal as you can.

Trigger	Going to a party and meeting new people
What happened	I drank too much and felt terrible the next day, worrying about what I said and did.
Plan for next time	Meet up with a friend for an alcohol-free dinner before the party. Agree a limit to the number of drinks I'll have at the party and don't exceed it. Or try going without drinking. If I choose not to drink at all, I will tell a trusted friend why I'm not drinking so she can help discreetly support me if people put pressure on me to drink. If I am feeling anxious at the party, I will just go home and have a bath, rather than staying and drinking more. Beforehand, I'll prepare some questions and topics of conversation to bring up with new people and some interesting news I can share about myself.

Trigger	Giving a presentation at work
What happened	I overthought it and put off preparing for it because it felt too daunting to tackle. I felt so unprepared on the day that I panicked and asked a colleague to cover for me.
Plan for next time	Instead of avoiding my fear of public speaking I will lean into it, step by step. Just making a start can help to make it feel less daunting and more manageable. Being prepared will give me confidence. I will begin by speaking up in small groups and then build up to larger presentations. Beforehand, instead of imagining all the things that could go wrong, I will visualize myself feeling at ease and confident, speaking slowly and clearly and breathing easily. I'll imagine feeling really proud of myself once it's over and getting positive feedback from my manager. I will be kind to myself no matter how it went and trust that it's a process and I will get better at it.

Trigger	Taking an exam
What happened	I crammed in the two weeks before the exam and I felt frazzled and anxious on the day.
Plan for next time	I will visualize myself on the day of the exam, walking calmly into the examination room, taking some deep breaths and calmly focusing on the exam paper. In the days and weeks leading up to it I will make time for relaxation and rest; making sure I have walks outside and plenty of study breaks, practising mindfulness and using worry time or speaking to a friend if I feel overwhelmed. I will prepare some mantras and affirmations to repeat to myself, such as, 'I know my stuff,' 'I am capable,' 'I feel confident.' In the examination room I will take some deep belly breaths and allow any nervous feeling to just be there. Then I will 'float' with the anxiety, without trying to make it stop.

Trigger	Heading to the gym for the first time
What happened	I went to the gym alone but ended up confused and nervous because I didn't know how to use the equipment and felt everyone was staring and judging me.
Plan for next time	I'll take a friend for support and book an induction with a gym instructor so that they can show us how to use all the equipment. I'll make sure I'm wearing my favourite leggings and focus on having fun with my friend. Even if I feel nervous or self-conscious, I'll stay with the feeling, knowing that I'll feel safer and more confident the more used to the gym I become.

Trigger

What
happened

Plan for
next time

Trigger

What
happened

Plan for
next time

Trigger

What
happened

Plan for
next time

Trigger	
What happened	
Plan for next time	

Brainstorm twenty ideas for activities that sum up self-care and relaxation for you.

✎ Examples:

Heading out for a walk in the park ....

Treating myself to a pedicure ....

Cooking a delicious meal at home ....

....

....

....

....

....

....

....

....

....

....

....

....

....

....

....

....

....

....

....

....

• •

Self-care diary

	Monday	Tuesday	Wednesday
morning	10 minutes of meditation		10 minutes of meditation
mid-morning			
lunchtime		walk in the park near the office	
mid-afternoon			
evening			

Thursday	Friday	Saturday	Sunday
	10 minutes of meditation	Yoga class	
Night in front of the TV			soak in the bath with Epsom salts

✎ Schedule in your self-care and relaxation time.
Try to do something each day.

	Monday	Tuesday	Wednesday
morning			
mid-morning			
lunchtime			
mid-afternoon			
evening			

Thursday	Friday	Saturday	Sunday

Q&A

Here are some answers to the questions I get asked most frequently by my clients and by women on social media.

It's Sunday night, I have a really important day at work tomorrow and I can't sleep. Aargh! What should I do?

Get out of bed and either read some fiction (a book, not on your phone!) for fifteen minutes, listen to a guided meditation or hypnosis audio (available at www.calmer-you.com/bonus), or do a body-scan muscle relaxation. Doing something calming and focused is often enough to distract you and calm you down so that you can sleep. Remind yourself that, no matter what Monday brings, you'll handle it. Some people find it helpful to do a 'brain dump' of worries and 'to-do's' to return to on Monday morning. Getting it down on paper can be a relief. For future, avoid coffee after lunchtime (caffeine takes ages to get out of your system) and do some exercise or yoga stretches to wear yourself out before you go to bed. I particularly like the yoga app Yin Yoga.

I just logged in to Instagram for five minutes . . .
that turned into an hour of checking out my
favourite beauty bloggers. Now I can't stop
comparing myself to these gorgeous women and
I'm an anxious wreck!

Firstly, if you know you have a tendency to 'compare and despair', it's worth curating who you follow so that you're less likely to be exposed to things that trigger insecurities. Un-follow anyone on Facebook and Instagram who makes you envious, angry or sad and try to make your social media feeds a place that lifts you up rather than one that brings you down. Remember that the glamour you see on celebrities' social media does not reflect how things are in real life and you can be certain that even these people have problems, too. Everyone feels crap sometimes, anxiety can affect anybody (even those who *look* perfect) and social media just isn't telling us the whole story. Remind yourself that you are unique; a one-time event in the universe with a special set of gifts and strengths. You have equal value to anyone else. Now, how can you start to focus on what's great about you and your life, instead of in what's lacking?

During the day I'm fine but when I get home
from work my mind goes into overdrive. How
can I stop overthinking everything?

Make your worrying as constructive as possible by applying the 'worry time' technique. Taking immediate action on your worries wherever possible will help, along with 'answering back' to worries in a calm and rational way. Practise being as mindful as you can with whatever you're doing; if you're cooking or cleaning, give it your full attention. Also spend some time thinking about what relaxes you and makes you happy and plan this into your evenings. Do you love to sing? Or do yoga? Does doing the pub quiz with your friends calm you down and light you up? Doing things that engage you and which you enjoy will help you to relax and take your mind off things. Also, I've said it before and I'll say it again: meditation. It changes your brain to make you calmer. Make it a priority.

Recently, a family member got sick. Now, every
time I feel an ache or a pain I imagine that
something is seriously wrong with me. Help!

When we're anxious, it's easy to catastrophize every bodily sensation and spiral into negative thoughts, but the fact is most aches and pains get better all by themselves. Your body is incredibly strong and resilient with an amazing ability to heal and repair itself. Try to switch your attention to all the ways, which your body is fabulous and healthy. Making a daily note of everything that works well can help you to tune into noticing all the evidence of your health. Doing some stream-of-consciousness writing about your anxieties and applying the 'worry time' techniques will also help.

I've been single for three years and I'm
thirty-five. I'm freaking out that I'll never
meet someone.

First off, I want to say that you are whole and valid just as you are and you don't need a partner to complete you. Also, it's easy to look at people in relationships and project on to them an idea of perfect happiness and harmony; which often isn't the case! Remember that you *can* be just as happy single, so don't wait for a partner before you'll allow yourself to be happy. Being single does *not* mean there's something wrong with you; you just haven't met the right person yet.

I know it's easier said than done, but try to be as relaxed and open as you can. Life contains infinite possibilities and focusing on what you want in a relaxed way is far more likely to help you get it than pushing and straining.

Instead of dwelling on what you don't have, focus on what's great about being single. Having the bed to yourself, girls' holidays and the freedom to do what the hell you like are just a few of the amazing things to enjoy when you're single. Everything has a season; there's a time to be single and there's a time for love. Trust that that time is coming.

Instead of worrying about it, think about what action you could take. Can you prioritize taking care of yourself so that, when you do meet someone, you're really ready for it? Or getting out and doing things you enjoy – which is a great way to meet like-minded people. Cherish this time to nurture yourself and have fun. You don't know when love could be just around the corner.

And remember, lots of women meet their partners and have babies in their late thirties and early forties. Janet Jackson has just announced her pregnancy aged fifty; Geri Halliwell at forty-four. There is enough time.

I've heard about self-soothing. What is it and how can I do it?

Self-soothing is all about calming your amygdala and therefore the fight-or-flight response. It's a term used in a type of therapy called Dialectical Behaviour Therapy and it basically refers to creating sensations to comfort yourself. Whenever we do something like breathing slowly and deeply, walking slowly and mindfully or having a massage, we're sending a message to our brain that we are safe and that there is no danger. Your brain can then get out of emergency mode and into relaxation mode. Usually, self-soothing activities are related to your senses: touch, taste, smell, sound and sight. I suggest making a list of the sorts of things that make you feel comforted and safe. Here are some ideas: stroking a pet, cooking a favourite meal, giving yourself a facial or a foot massage, curling up on the sofa with a blanket, looking at the clouds, singing or listening to music or sipping a warm milky drink. Try different things and notice what works for you.

> I have social anxiety and it seems to be getting worse. I fear going out and meeting people and it means I end up staying in alone.
> What can I do?

Firstly, it's important to work on your self-esteem. Be kind to yourself, do things you love to do and which are good at and frequently remind yourself of everything that's good about you. If you don't feel good about yourself, you're more likely to be affected by the judgements and criticisms of other people. If you have a strong sense of your own worth and value, it creates a buffer against external factors so that things are less likely to affect you. Remember that criticism and judgements by other people are inevitable for all of us from time to time and often not about you anyway, but rather about how the other person views you through their own filter.

Secondly, examine the thoughts and beliefs you have about yourself and your situation. Do you believe you should be perfect all the time in order to be accepted by others? Do you expect that you should be liked by every-one? Practise 'answering back' kindly and rationally to these thoughts. The more you practise this, the more you create new neural pathways in your brain that will help you to automatically think about things in a more helpful way. Be kind to yourself and see yourself as an always evolving, intrinsically lovable person.

Finally, although the anxiety makes you want to hide away, try to challenge yourself, lean into the fear and do things that push you out of your comfort zone. Your amygdala will eventually get the message that other people aren't actually dangerous and you'll find that your confidence will grow.

I have a phobia of heights that really affects my life. I'd love to be able to go up in glass lifts to sip cocktails on a roof terrace or to climb mountains, but I'm terrified!

Phobias are a very specific type of anxiety where your brain associates a certain trigger with danger. Often, there is an initial triggering event whereby, for example, you had a fright while up a mountain and your brain associated the feeling of fear with height. The phobia is a way of trying to keep you safe from danger in the future. The other way that phobias can develop is through learning, maybe from a parent or other family member who had a similar fear. Either way, phobias are learnt and they can therefore be unlearnt. Good news!

The most commonly used technique for overcoming a phobia is gradual exposure. It's usually best to get the help of a therapist or hypnotherapist to do this, but you could try it yourself if you feel able to.

Start by just doing this in your imagination. Take some deep breaths (or do the guided meditation available at www.calmer-you.com/bonus) to get nice and relaxed. Then imagine yourself enjoying a drink on a roof terrace, or feeling great as you climb a mountain. Use all your senses to imagine how you'll feel, what you'll see and think, the smells, tastes and sensations. If it makes you anxious, imagine you are seeing it on a screen at first, then step into the screen when you feel calm enough to do so. With enough practice, you teach your mind that the situation is safe. Once you're comfortable with this, take it into the real world. Start off with small challenges, such as going up one floor in a glass lift, or climbing a small hill. Use relaxation techniques such as 3–5 breathing to calm yourself down as you do it. Even if you experience some fear, try to stay with the feeling and breathe through it. Staying with the fear teaches your amygdala that the situation is safe. Slowly build up to bigger hills and higher floors in the lift until you feel really confident.

My partner wants to support me when I'm really anxious but he doesn't know what to do. Is there anything you can suggest?

Firstly, I'd recommend asking them to learn as much about anxiety as possible. Sometimes, people who haven't experienced anxiety think you should be able to 'snap out of it' but, as we know, that's not the way it works. Explain exactly what having anxiety is like and encourage them to read about other people's experiences on blogs or sites such as Mind or Anxiety UK; the more understanding they have, the more they'll be able to empathize. If they've been trying to force you out of your comfort zone before you're ready, let them know that this just makes you more anxious.

Lastly, tell them how they can support and help you. Maybe you just need someone to listen without judgement, or perhaps your partner can come along with you to an appointment with your GP or therapist. Sometimes, there is nothing anyone can do other than simply be with you, which is support in itself.

I always get super-anxious just before my period. Is there anything I can do about this?

Hormonal fluctuations around the time of your period can certainly make anxiety symptoms worse but there are a few things you can do to relieve them. Most of the advice in the chapter about eating to beat anxiety also applies to managing the symptoms of PMS anxiety.

Firstly, try to eat little and often. Keeping your blood-sugar levels steady will help you to feel more balanced overall. So no matter how busy you are – don't forget to eat!

There is some evidence[12] to suggest that taking a supplement of magnesium and vitamin B6 could help with the symptoms of PMS. A study done in 2013 found that omega-3 fatty acids helped to reduce the psychiatric effects of PMS.[13] Things like exercising and avoiding coffee, alcohol and sugar may also help.

> I feel like my to-do list is never-ending. As soon as I tick one thing off, five more things are added to it. How can I stop feeling so overwhelmed?

If my mind is feeling overloaded, I remind myself of this quote from self-help author and teacher Byron Katie: 'What we need to do unfolds before us, always – doing the dishes, paying the bills, picking up the children's socks, brushing our teeth. We never receive more than we can handle, and there is always just one thing to do. Life never gets more difficult than that.' The only time that anything can be done is in the present moment. It might feel as if your to-do list is piling up on top of you, but the only thing you need to do is whatever you're doing right now.

Make a list of things to do in the future and leave them there until you have to address them. What you're doing right now is all that is required of you and you have all the resources and abilities to deal with it, in this moment.

In his book *Supercoach*, Michael Neill suggests we have two to-do lists: one with all the things we'd like to do in a day and another with just one major thing we have to do right now. Once you've completed that one thing, move another item on to the 'one thing' list. That way, you've only ever got one thing to do, and it's less overwhelming!

Resources

Online help

http://www.mind.org.uk/ – the Mental Health Charity

www.anxietyuk.org.uk – a charity for those with anxiety, providing information, support and services. Call their (UK) info line (08444 775 774) for support from someone who's suffered with anxiety between Monday and Friday, 9.30 a.m. to 5.30 p.m

www.rethink.org – help and support for people affected by mental illness

http://www.time-to-change.org.uk – a growing movement of people changing how we all think about and act towards mental-health problems

www.citizensadvice.org.uk – provides free, confidential information and advice to help people sort out their money, and with legal, consumer and other problems

www.samaritans.org – available twenty-four hours a day to provide confidential emotional support for people who are experiencing feelings of distress, despair or suicidal thoughts. Telephone: 116 123 (UK)

NHS 111 Service – dial 111 when you need medical help but it's not an emergency.

https://www.b-eat.co.uk/ – Beat is the UK's leading charity supporting anyone affected by eating disorders, anorexia, bulimia, EDNOS or any other difficulties with food, weight and body shape

Further reading

The Happiness Advantage: The Seven Principles of Positive Psychology That Fuel Success and Performance at Work by Shawn Achor (Virgin Books)

When Perfect Isn't Good Enough: Strategies for Coping with Perfectionism by Martin Antony and Richard Swinson (New Harbinger Publications)

The Gifts of Imperfection: Let Go of Who You Think You're Supposed to Be and Embrace Who You Are by Brene Brown (Hazelden)

Feeling Good: The New Mood Therapy by Dr David Burns (Harper)

The Chimp Paradox: The Mind-management Programme to Help You Achieve Success, Confidence and Happiness by Professor Steve Peters (Vermilion)

Mindfulness: A Practical Guide to Finding Peace in a Frantic World by Mark Williams and Dr Danny Penman (Piatkus)

Cook. Nourish. Glow. by Amelia Freer (Michael Joseph)

Meditation and yoga

http://uk.tm.org/ – find out where you can learn transcendental meditation (TM)

www.calmer-you.com/bonus – download a free guided meditation and a hypnotherapy audio track for relaxation

Headspace app – mindfulness meditation that starts with just ten minutes a day

Buddhify app – more than eighty guided meditations to choose from

Omvana app – guided meditations for relaxation and focus

Yin Yoga app – gentle yoga to help you to relax and sleep

Everyday Yoga for Stress Release with Nadia Narain (DVD)

Check out your local Buddhist or yoga centre; they will probably offer meditation classes

References

Chapter 2. Why are we all so worried?

1. https://www.mentalhealth.org.uk/publications/living-with-anxiety
2. http://onlinelibrary.wiley.com/doi/10.1002/brb3.497/abstract
3. http://www.ncbi.nlm.nih.gov/pubmed/1537781
4. https://www.ncbi.nlm.nih.gov/pubmed/16688123
5. http://hrccatalog.hrrh.on.ca/InmagicGenie/DocumentFolder/copinganxietyphobias.pdf
6. https://www.gov.uk/government/news/research-finds-women-paid-less-than-men-in-90-of-sectors
7. http://www.sciencedirect.com/science/article/pii/S0272735809000671
8. https://www.theguardian.com/lifeandstyle/2013/mar/14/women-experience-stress-work-research
9. http://link.springer.com/article/10.1007%2Fs10826-013-9716-3
10. http://journals.plos.org/plosone/article?id=10.1371/journal.pone.0139004
11. http://www.happinessresearchinstitute.com

12. http://www.sciencedirect.com/science/article/pii/S0191886909001226
13. http://psp.sagepub.com/content/38/9/1133.abstract
14. https://www.anxietyuk.org.uk/get-involved/
15. Office for National Statistics 'Surveys of psychiatric morbidity in Great Britain. Report 1 – the prevalence of psychiatric morbidity among adults living in private households', The Stationery Office, 1995
16. http://www.ncbi.nlm.nih.gov/pubmed/10641368
17. https://ourworldindata.org/

Chapter 3. Anxiety: your biggest teacher

1. http://www.nature.com/neuro/journal/v7/n8/full/nn1276.html
2. https://bbrfoundation.org/brain-matters-discoveries/creative-scientist-explores-the-brain-and-discovers-its-%E2%80%9Cplasticity%E2%80%9D

Chapter 4. Boosting self-esteem

1. https://yougov.co.uk/news/2015/07/21/over-third-brits-unhappy-their-bodies-celebrity-cu/
2. Striegel-Moore, R., Franko, D. 'Body image issues among girls and women' in Cash, T.F. and Pruzinsky, T. (eds.), *Body Image: A Handbook of Theory, Research, and Clinical Practice*, New York: Guilford Press, pp. 183–91
3. Tiggemann, M. 'Media exposure, body dissatisfaction and disordered eating: Television and magazines are

not the same!', *European Eating Disorders Review*, 11(5) (2003), pp. 418–30

4. Becker, Anne E. *Body, Self, and Society: The View from Fiji*, University of Pennsylvania Press, 1995
5. Model Alliance Survey http://modelalliance.org/industry-analysis
6. Neff, K. D. and McGeehee, P. 'Self-compassion and psychological resilience among adolescents and young adults', *Self and Identity*, 9 (2010), pp. 225–40

Chapter 5. Decisions, decisions

1. http://www.apa.org/helpcenter/willpower.aspx
2. http://www.jneurosci.org/content/36/11/3322.abstract
3. Woods, A. 'Get excited: reappraising pre-performance anxiety as excitement', *Journal of Experimental Psychology* (2013)
4. http://www.ncbi.nlm.nih.gov/pmc/articles/PMC4359724/

Chapter 7. It's all about the brain – not the ass!

1. http://cel.webofknowledge.com
2. http://journal.frontiersin.org/article/10.3389/fpsyt.2013.00027/full
3. http://www.jneurosci.org/content/33/18/7770.abstract
4. Duman, R. S. 'Regulation of adult neurogenesis by

antidepressant treatment', *Neuropsychopharmacology*, 25 (2001), pp. 836–44

5. Broman-Fulks, J. J. and Storey, K. M. 'Evaluation of a brief aerobic exercise intervention for high anxiety sensitivity', *Anxiety Stress Coping*, 21 (2008), pp. 117–28
6. https://www.psy.ox.ac.uk/publications/298164
7. http://www.ncbi.nlm.nih.gov/pmc/articles/ PMC3939966/
8. http://www.ncbi.nlm.nih.gov/pubmed
9. http://www.mind.org.uk/news-campaigns/news/ new-research-shows-benefits-of-ecotherapy-for- mental-health-and-wellbeing
10. http://www.ncbi.nlm.nih.gov/pmc/articles/ PMC1725091/

Chapter 8. Eating to beat anxiety

1. http://www.sciencedirect.com/science/article/pii/ S0166223613000088
2. Mitsuoka, T. 'Intestinal flora and aging', *Nutrition Reviews*, 50 (1992), pp. 438–46
3. http://www.ncbi.nlm.nih.gov/pubmed/20696216
4. Allen, A. P. et al. 'Towards psychobiotics for stress & cognition: Bifidobacterium longum blocks stress-induced behavioural and physiology changes and modulates brain activity and neurocognitive performance in healthy human subjects', https:// www.isge.ie/abstracts/view/124
5. http://www.ncbi.nlm.nih.gov/pubmed/21040780

References

6. http://www.ncbi.nlm.nih.gov/pmc/articles/PMC4410136

7. Mantovani, A. (2008) 'Inflammation and cancer', http://www.nature.com/nature/journal/v454/n7203/full/nature07205.html)

8. Willerson, J. T. and Ridker, P. M. (2004), 'Inflammation and heart disease', http://circ.ahajournals.org/content/109/21_suppl_1/II-2

9. Salim, S. et al. (2013) http://www.ncbi.nlm.nih.gov/pubmed/22814704

10. Kiecolt-Glaser, J. K. et al. http://www.ncbi.nlm.nih.gov/pubmed/21784145

11. http://www.bjmp.org/content/irritable-bowel-syndrome-primary-care-physicians

12. https://www.ncbi.nlm.nih.gov/pubmed/27382323

13. http://www.ncbi.nlm.nih.gov/pubmed/2195579

14. http://www.ncbi.nlm.nih.gov/pubmed/2835648

15. http://www.sciencedirect.com/science/article/pii/S0165178108001911

16. Lu, Ting et al. (2012) http://www.nrjournal.com/article/S0271-5317(12)00102-9/abstract

17. https://www.ncbi.nlm.nih.gov/pubmed/1844561

18. https://www.ncbi.nlm.nih.gov/pmc/articles/PMC3208934/

19. https://www.ncbi.nlm.nih.gov/pubmed/26680471

20. https://www.ncbi.nlm.nih.gov/pmc/articles/PMC506781

21. https://www.ncbi.nlm.nih.gov/pmc/articles/PMC506781

Chapter 9. The Anxiety Solution Toolkit

1. http://tmhome.com/experiences/katy-perry-singer/
2. 62 http://tmhome.com/experiences/tm-meditation-for-cameron-diaz/
3. Goldin, P. R., and Gross, J. J. 'Effects of mindfulness-based stress reduction (MBSR) on emotion regulation in social anxiety disorder', *Emotion*, 10 (2010), pp. 1, 83–91
4. Kabat-Zinn, J. et al 'Effectiveness of a meditation-based stress reduction program in the treatment of anxiety disorders', *American Journal of Psychiatry*, 149 (1992), pp. 936–43
5. http://www.ncbi.nlm.nih.gov/pmc/articles/PMC1361002/
6. Dillbeck M. C. 'The effect of the transcendental meditation technique on anxiety level', *Journal of Clinical Psychology*, 33 (1977), pp. 1076–78
7. Schneider R. H. 'Altered responses of cortisol, GH, TSH and testosterone to acute stress after four months' practice of transcendental meditation (TM)', *Annals of the New York Academy of Sciences*, 746 (1994), pp. 381–4
8. http://uk.tm.org/stress-and-the-brain
9. http://www.ncbi.nlm.nih.gov/pubmed/22291847
10. https://www.psychologytoday.com/blog/sapient-nature/201310/how-negative-is-your-mental-chatter

References

11. https://www.ncbi.nlm.nih.gov/pmc/articles/
    PMC3010965
12. https://www.ncbi.nlm.nih.gov/pmc/articles/
    PMC3208934/
13. https://www.ncbi.nlm.nih.gov/pubmed/23642943

Index